PATHS AND STORIES

Kevin Treston

PATHS AND STORIES

Spirituality for teachers and catechists

VERITAS

Published 1991 by
Veritas Publicatons
7-8 Lower Abbey Street
Dublin 1

First published 1988 by Creation Enterprises
3 Hogan Court
Samford Q 4520
Australia

Copyright © Creation Enterprises 1988, 1991

ISBN 1 85390 162 8

Scripture quotes are taken from the Jerusalem Bible, published and copyright © 1966, 1967 and 1968 by Darton, Longman and Todd Ltd and Doubleday and Co. Inc., and are used by permission of the publishers.

Cover Design by Banahan McManus
Typesetting by Typeform, Dublin
Printed by Betaprint, Dublin

Contents

Introduction 5

1. Beginnings 7
2. Why spirituality for teachers now? 21
3. The heritage of spirituality 30
4. Jesus the teacher 40
5. The teacher as a creation person 53
6. Teachers and the cross 66
7. The teacher as a caring person 74
8. The teacher as one who is called 86
9. Continuing the journey 98

Sayings of consolation 115

Bibliography 117

INTRODUCTION

Early in my life, I felt called to be a teacher. Now after over thirty years of teaching, I'm grateful to God for the vocation of being a teacher. I'm thankful for the grace of teaching and having been taught by so many students during these years. As I write this book, the memory of many student faces accompanies me through these pages.

Paths and Stories has been written to assist teachers in developing a spirituality for themselves in their vocation of being teachers. Although I write from the personal position of being Catholic, I hope the ecumenical flavour of this book will make it relevant for all those engaged in Christian teaching, such as staffs of Catholic schools, CCD, Sunday school teachers, adult educators, priests and ministers. A teacher is one who is engaged in the work of education.

The word 'education' is derived from the Latin word *educare*, meaning a 'drawing out' of the gifts of the other. Teaching is a relational activity and is concerned with the communication of the human story and wisdoms of the world. A teacher walks a little way along the life journeys of the students. The title *Paths and Stories* attempts to capture the spirit of a teacher's spirituality. There are many paths on the way to God and countless stories which may be told about the mystery of meeting God on the way.

A Christian teacher is invited to share her or his encounter with Jesus and his Kingdom. John's gospel records a meeting between Jesus and two curious followers:

> Jesus turned round, saw them following and said, 'What do you want? They answered 'Rabbi' – which means Teacher – 'Where do you live?' 'Come and see' he replied; so they went and saw where he lived, and stayed with him the rest of that day (Jn 1:37-39).

Introduction

The three verbs in verse 39 are significant for an exploration of a spirituality of a teacher:

'went' – a person needs to follow a quest, a journey of the spiritual life;

'saw' – implies a search for truth, wisdom and right priorities;

'stayed' – suggests that a person must spend some time with the Lord, in observing, reflecting and responding.

Paths and Stories is intended as a resource book for people to reflect on the various aspects of a teacher's spirituality.

There are three sections to each chapter:

- **Content:** Insights into spirituality according to a theme
- **Reflection:** Questions or exercises to consider
- **Scripture:** Passages which have been chosen as appropriate sources of meditation on the theme of each chapter.

Because God's presence in the life of each person has its own unique expression, the Content, Reflection and Scripture will evoke different responses within each person according to her or his consciousness and spiritual aspirations.

May *Paths and Stories* be a contribution to the lives of Christian educators!

I wish to express my sincere thanks to my wife Kathryn for her support and critical advice, also to Glenda Rodgers, Sr Pauline Burke and Peter Gagen for their comments on the text. Thanks too to the Marist Brothers for their educational wisdom and heritage of spirituality which has influenced my own spiritual life.

Kevin Treston
Brisbane
Australia

1

BEGINNINGS

Once upon a time a man grew tired of his family and little town. So he set off for a journey to Magic City. He travelled many miles until he grew weary and lay down to sleep. To make sure he knew the way to Magic City, he left his shoes outside the sleeping place pointing in the direction of his destination. During the night a trickster came along and turned his shoes around the other way. Next morning the traveller continued the way pointed by his shoes until he arrived at the town. He was so excited to be in Magic City. He explored the buildings, marvelling at the parks and the people. Eventually he came to a lovely little house which seemed vaguely familiar. He went inside and realised he had returned to his house, his family and his town. He rejoiced because he truly had come home again. And it seemed so different, so new!

Spirituality for a teacher is like this story. We become so familiar with our task as teachers, our teaching styles may become routine, our classes may be boring. Perhaps we need to travel away from our familiar places to seek a Magic City of spirituality so that we may return again to our place of teaching with excitement and enlightenment.

The meaning of spirituality and the role of a Christian teacher are two key themes which are examined throughout this book. Today we hear a great deal about 'spirituality'. For some people the very word conjures up images of ponderous religious dogma, rigid Christian rituals and something belonging to another era. Spirituality might be considered the preserve of rather holy people who have made a deep commitment to God. Even for catechists, teachers in Catholic schools and adult educators, there might be some reservations about taking seriously a call to develop further a spirituality appropriate for teachers. Yet for any teacher engaged in Christian education, spirituality is at the heart of this endeavour. Spirituality is an expression of a teacher's values and beliefs about God and human life.

A teacher is one who is involved in transformation. This transformation includes a committed action to extend the possibilities and potential of her or his students, to lead students' visions to new horizons and to empower them to realise the gifts they possess as human people. Teaching is about transformation of values, knowledge, attitudes to justice and citizenship. It challenges the students to travel beyond the boundaries which have been set by environment, by schooling, by culture and self-concepts. Transforming Christian education invites students to imagine other ways of living and being. Such education is transforming if it leads people to a new relationship with the world, with one another and with God.

Teachers in a Catholic school constitute a key activating group in that educational community. The religious heart of the Catholic school is the presence of Christ lived by the people of the school community. Catholic schools claim to offer an education which is holistic, that is, integrating the secular and religious dimensions of life. In the USSC document *To Teach as Jesus Did* (1972), we read:

> The integration of religious truth and values with the rest of life is brought about in the Catholic school not only by its unique curriculum, but more importantly, by the presence of teachers who express an integrated approach to learning and living in their private and professional lives. It is further reinforced by free interaction among the students within their own community of youth. (104)

The task of integrating the secular and religious is one which requires a conversion to a religious way of perceiving reality. It seems to imply a religious view of the world as well as an openness to the wisdoms of education and learning generally. If we regard the integration of religion and life as a key role for Catholic schools, then the question of spirituality for teachers is surely a foundational one.

In this era of Catholic schools, virtually the whole of the staff is lay. On any staff today, there is usually a wide pluralism of beliefs among Catholic and other staff members. Whatever happens about spirituality must be real and relevant for these people. The language used in presentations and readings about spirituality should accord with the levels of readiness of the staff. For catechists and adult religious educators, Sunday school teachers, spirituality for teachers has many common elements with teachers from Catholic schools.

Meaning of spirituality

The word 'spirituality' needs to be explored so that teachers may locate their own understanding of the term as it arises out of their particular vocation of teaching. The concept of spirituality may evoke a variety of reactions from interest to passivity or even resistance. Spirituality may be associated with a committed Christian life style which is more often identified with that of ministers, priests or religious sisters and brothers. Such misconceptions might be blocks to teachers who may feel that spirituality is not really for them.

A Christian teacher does not begin in a vacuum in approaching the topic of spirituality. There is a rich heritage of almost two thousand years of writing about spirituality from which we may draw inspiration and wisdom. The countless stories of men and women throughout the Christian era give testimony to its diversity and creativity.

Paths and Stories

To appreciate the meaning of spirituality, we need to examine its many expressions and descriptions. These various perspectives on spirituality will assist us in offering themes for a spirituality for Christian teachers.

Spirituality may be regarded as a search for God in the everyday events of life so that we may be brought into a new wholeness of our being. Spirituality is an endeavour to become more fully a woman or man in the Spirit. Jesus announced his mission as:

> I have come
> so that they may have life
> and have it to the full (Jn 10:10).

Spirituality is not something added to our humanity, it is of the very essence of what it means to be human.

The word 'spirituality' is derived from the Latin word *spirare,* meaning to breathe. The word suggests the creative movement of the Spirit bringing forth life as the Spirit of God created light from darkness (Gn 1:3) This wind of God *(ruah)* is described by Jesus:

> The wind blows wherever it pleases;
> you hear its sound,
> but you cannot tell where it comes from or where it is going.
> That is how it is with all who are born of the Spirit
> (Jn 3:8).

There is a mystery in how God acts in our lives but we seek to allow the gentle breeze of the Spirit to create within us. The story of one's Christian life can then be perceived as a series of rebirthings, new creatings of the Spirit.

Spirituality is a style of living which assists the realisation of our potential to be created in the image of God. It is a quest to bring to fulfilment the God-likeness to us. Spirituality involves a process of divinisation, becoming like God.

Spirituality is not simply a solitary quest to save one's soul. All Christian spirituality is relational and has a communal dimension. I cannot simply confine my relationships with God to myself. If the encounter with the Lord does not flow out into reflective action of compassion, there is something false in its direction. Our relationship with God is interwoven with our interactions with our sisters and brothers of the world.

Our cultural environment is the context of the character of our spiritual life. Spirituality establishes a new communion with the earth. The world is not a booby-trapped battleground but a sacrament of God's presence in creation.

Spirituality involves our whole person in our experiences with life. The spiritual life is not the business of the soul while the body is somewhere else. Such dichotomy is foreign to the oneness of being a human person. In the first letter of John we read:

> Something which has existed since the beginning,
> that we have heard,
> and we have seen with our own eyes;
> that we have watched
> and touched with our hands;
> the Word who is life –
> this is our subject (1 Jn 1:1-4).

Our response to God's loving invitations may be manifested in prayer or worship but for most of the time, the spiritual life is realised through ordinary happenings of our daily routine, such as: eating, teaching, gardening, cooking, taking the children to sport, washing, watching TV and relating to the family and the school community.

There is a profound mystery in the sanctity of the

ordinary. Jesus spent 90 per cent of his life at Nazareth engaged in simple labour. Only in the last few years did he engage in a public ministry of teaching and preaching. In the age of the spectacular, we may perhaps forget the graced moment of the everyday. Spirituality, as John reminds us, is a total experience of our beings. It is not a mere intellectual or feeling response. God's graciousness is to our whole being. There is no place for dualism in Christian spirituality. God does not speak to the soul only but to the body/soul being as a fully human person.

The incarnational feature of spirituality cannot be too strongly emphasised because even the word 'spirituality' may suggest a meaning of 'belonging to the spirit world' or 'not real'. Yet the answer to the question: 'What does it mean to live given the fact that one day I will die?' is probably one of the most profound (and real) issues which a person will face. Spirituality is described as set in 'the market place' to situate God's call to holiness within the context of everyday events. The slogan 'bloom where you are planted' might be an apt comment for market-place spirituality.

Baptism is the sacrament of initiation into the Christian community. Spirituality is a living out of the possibilities of being baptised. Through Baptism, Christians are set free to live as daughters and sons of God:

> The spirit you received is not the spirit of slaves bringing fear into your lives again; it is the spirit of sons, and it makes us cry out 'Abba, Father!' The Spirit himself and our spirit bear united witness that we are children of God. And if we are children we are heirs as well: heirs of God and coheirs of Christ, sharing his sufferings so as to share his Glory (Rm 8:14-17).

By becoming members of the Christian community through Baptism, the person hopefully will experience this community as an important source of energy for spirituality.

Christian spirituality has an ecclesial dimension. One person's spirituality is in communion with the gifts of the spirit within the Christian community. The story of one member of the Church joins the chorus of stories of countless stories of spirituality. The Church should be a nourishing mother for its members so that the community of disciples experience God's saving mercy and love within a group which challenges and supports. Although some Christians do not find the Church a significant agency in their spiritual lives, that does not lessen the urgency of promoting the importance of a viable Christian community for spirituality.

Spirituality involves some kind of conversion or 'metanoia'. Conversion is not a one-event thing or instant happening on Christ but rather a series of reorientations to recognise God as the centre of our being. This necessitates many struggles to incorporate what happens on the life journey into some kind of personal coherence. At the bottom line, we must utter a series of faith expressions in the fact that God always desires our happiness. We get lots of apparent evidence to the contrary. 'How could this happen to me, to her, to them?' is an all too common cry of anguish. St Paul reminds us that somehow every event can be transformed into a step on the pathway to God if we have faith:

> We know that by turning everything to their good,
> God co-operates with all those who love him (Rm 8:28).

We make choices about our spiritual life. The Adam and Eve story describes the consequences of choosing (Gn 3). Freedom to choose a life stance towards God or away from God is inherent in the nature of being a human person. The parable of the sower and the seed (Mk 4:1-10) suggests six positions which anyone may take in response to the word of God. At one extreme, a person disregards the word, symbolised by the birds taking the seeds. At the other extreme is the fruitfulness of the person who responds fully to the word and harvests a hundredfold.

In the succession of choices we make along the way, Christians seek to cling in faith to the belief that God loves us. The coming of Jesus was the climax of this love for the world:

> Yes, God loved the world so much
> that he gave his only Son,
> so that everyone who believes in him may not be lost
> but may have eternal life (Jn 3:16).

The question of choice is critical in appreciating one's spirituality. No one can force us to be spiritual. The school, parish and educational system cannot demand that we be spiritual people. We cannot be bludgeoned into sanctity. Spirituality is a choice to engage in God's gift of graciousness.

There are many other descriptions of spirituality:

- the way a person lives out her or his ideals as a religious person;
- becoming what God hopes we will become;
- the way in which we are present to ourselves, to God and to our world;
- discovering the transcendence of God through the mystery of being;
- allowing God to transform our lives.

From the various descriptions of spirituality, some common themes emerge.

Spirituality is:
- a journey
- a discovery
- a response in faith
- a search for ultimate meaning
- an engagement in relationships
- discipleship
- being companioned by the Spirit
- becoming whole in holiness
- entering more fully the creative action of the Spirit
- living our Baptism as Christians
- encountering Jesus
- developing our capacity in faith, hope and love
- nurturing the relational dimension of our life.

Our own spiritual journey is special to us. Our name is written on it. Our personality type, our culture environment, our ethnic roots, religious formation, teaching situation, family relationships, are some of the influences which shape the direction and style of our spirituality. The Exodus theme, which is so central to the message of the Hebrew scriptures, is an appropriate one for the spiritual way. We follow many paths in faith on this journey. But faith is a gift from God and we learn to wait patiently for the graciousness of the Lord to touch us.

God works through our personal maturation. When we were young, our faith growth was dependent on parents and teachers. As we grew older we began to ask questions, to challenge others and ourselves in our beliefs. As adults, we may have taken a personal faith stance which is closely affiliated with a Church or we may pursue a faith life which is not energised by any Church group.

The symbol of the mustard seed offers an image of the word's power to continue growing within us. The parable describes the seed of discipleship:

> Night and day, while he sleeps, when he is awake, the seed is sprouting and growing; how he does not know (Mk 4:27).

The phrase 'night and day' is rather encouraging for us. We can feel very discouraged that we don't seem to be changing in our spirituality, just drifting along. We may often feel dry and without any religious faith at all. God seems light years away from what is happening in our life. Yet these periods of religious inactivity may be new springs of spiritual water. We don't quite understand how it happens, but for those of faith, the *Spirit* keeps moving in, 'how he does not know'. In faith, we need to jolt our consciousness that the hidden Lord is walking beside us as he travelled with the bewildered disciples on the way to Emmaus (Lk 24:13-35).

There are various rhythms and seasons for each person. All of us experience seasons of winter, when we lose heart, summer when we bask in the heat of life, autumn, when we sense something is dying within us, and spring, when we are energised by life. These passages are opportunities for growth. We cross various thresholds. Our point of reality is our moment of grace. God's gift of life is present at each phase of living, when we laugh, cry, celebrate or travel. The cycle of what is happening is described in Ecclesiastes:

> There is a season for everything, a time for every occupation under heaven;
> A time for giving birth,
> a time for dying;
> a time for planting,
> a time for uprooting what has been planted.

A time for killing,
a time for healing;
a time for knocking down,
a time for building.
A time for tears,
a time for laughter;
a time for mourning,
a time for dancing.
A time for throwing stones away,
a time for gathering them up;
a time for embracing
a time for searching
a time for losing;
a time for keeping,
a time for throwing away.
A time for tearing,
a time for sewing;
a time for keeping silent,
a time for speaking.
A time for loving,
a time for hating;
a time for war,
a time for peace (Qo 3:1-8).

Spirituality is letting the Lord of the journey be a presence in the paradox of our times.

Paths and Stories

REFLECTION

1. Which words or phrases express what spirituality means for you (e.g. journey, responding)?

2. Who (what) has been significant in influencing your spiritual life?

   What are the helping and limiting factors in your spiritual life now (e.g. atmosphere of the school, family)?

Helping	Limiting

3. In what ways does being a teacher (teacher in a Catholic school, CCD, adult educator, Sunday school teacher) affect your spiritual life?

4. How might you discover God in your teaching vocation?

SCRIPTURE

Mark 4:26-29

Jesus also said, 'This is what the kingdom of God is like. A man throws seed on the land. Night and day, while he sleeps, when he is awake, the seed is sprouting and growing; how, he does not know. Of its own accord the land produces first the shoot, then the ear, then the full grain in the ear. And when the crop is ready, he loses no time; he starts to reap because the harvest has come.'

Deuteronomy 1:29-33

'And I said to you: Do not take fright, do not be afraid of them. Yahweh your God goes in front of you and will be fighting on your side as you saw him fight for you in Egypt. In the wilderness, too, you saw him: how Yahweh carried you, as a man carries his child, all along the road you travelled on the way to this place. But for all this, you put no faith in Yahweh your God, who had gone in front of you on the journey to find you a camping ground, by night in the fire to light your path, by day in the cloud.'

Mark 1:9-11

It was at this time that Jesus came from Nazareth in Galilee and was baptised in the Jordan by John. No sooner had he come up out of the water than he saw the heavens torn apart and the Spirit, like a dove, descending on him. And a voice came from heaven, 'You are my Son, the Beloved; my favour rests on you.'

1 Corinthians 1:4-9

I never stop thanking God for all the graces you have received through Jesus Christ. I thank him that you have been enriched in so many ways, especially in your teachers and preachers; the witness to Christ has indeed been strong among you so that you will not be without any of the gifts of the Spirit while you are waiting for our Lord Jesus Christ to be revealed; and he will keep you steady and without blame until the last day, the day of our Lord Jesus Christ, because God by calling you has joined you to his Son, Jesus Christ; and God is faithful.

2

WHY SPIRITUALITY FOR TEACHERS NOW?

I believe that many influences have brought a new consciousness about an appreciation of spirituality and more particularly a spirituality for teachers in Christian education. This chapter will examine some of the factors which have generated a new focus on the topic of Christian spirituality.

Culture
Our world has undergone a succession of dramatic changes during the past century. The twentieth century has witnessed the horrors of two world wars, the depression, and a growing crisis in ecology. New ideologies such as communism, fascism, capitalism and scientific socialism have taken form in political systems which have undermined human dignity. The social sciences, especially psychology, anthropology and sociology, have made tremendous contributions to our understanding of the human condition. Christianity has sought to adapt its message and pastoral structures to this new world of the computer and electronic media. Traditional meaning systems have crumbled before a revolution in values. Contemporary religious groups are searching for a new story which will communicate religious values within a new consciousness. Spirituality for today must mediate transcendent meaning within a context of scientific materialism. Who is God among the vociferous shouts for money-making schemes? Who is God for people who live below the poverty line? Where do we discover the

revolutionary dream of Jesus among the dreams of Lotto and the golden casket? What is the image of the Christian Churches among the people? Do we need new models of spirituality to resonate with the pulse of our society or do we adopt a spirituality which is counter-cultural to the scramble of materialism?

Social justice
The relationship between spirituality and the social context of society raises questions about relevance to society. The increasing gap between rich and poor in our country and in the world generally, disturbs our consciences and causes us to reflect on the direction of our spiritual endeavours. Is the spiritual life a kind of angelic ego trip? The 'other world' view of spirituality was characterised by a flight from the world and emphasised the soul rather than the whole person. 'Good works' were encouraged as a consequence of this 'soul' spirituality. But the 'good works' were regarded as a condition of entry into heaven, not an integral dimension of the spiritual life. This brand of spirituality was individualistic and introspective. Today authentic Christian spirituality implies a conversion to social ethical actions and a commitment to social justice.

Ecumenism
Christian spirituality in the last few decades has been enriched by the interchange of insights among various Christian Churches and by an increasing openness to the wisdom of eastern religions. Although commercial and imperial activities dominated the early stages of western incursions into the East, religious interactions occurred more frequently as the twentieth century progressed. Western Christian missionaries began to modify their earlier dismissal of Hinduism and Buddhism and developed a respect for the profundity of religious thought. More recently, Christian spirituality has been transformed

by learning from the teachings of Zen, Sufi, Hinduism and Taoism. The Eastern proverb, 'Lose the mind and come to your senses', has found an echo in many contemporary spiritualities. Protestant and Catholic traditions of spirituality have been shared in ecumenical church meetings and prayer gatherings. The ecumenical climate has led to an appreciation of how the Spirit moves hearts in very diverse cultural environments.

Holistic attitudes
Modern psychology has demonstrated the essential oneness of the human person. Many ancient cultures, including the Jewish one, taught the unity of human beings. However, the mainstream of Christian spirituality was affected by dualistic views of humanity, that body and soul were separate entities. Heresies such as Gnosticism and Jansenism taught this dichotomy between body and soul. Such theories stressed the soul as the object of spiritual activity with a corresponding disregard for the body. Contemporary spirituality gradually incorporated the theories of the social sciences about the oneness of the human person and returned to a more holistic approach in the spiritual life. 'Holiness' is a description for a coming to wholeness. Thus advice by spiritual directors about prayer and asceticism is now integrated into concern for rest and exercise.

 Related to this dualism within the human person was the gradual separation between theology and spirituality. By the late Middle Ages, a serious rift had developed between theology as an intellectual study and spirituality as a personal devotional exercise. Both theology and spirituality were impoverished by this split. Theology became more speculative and theoretical. It lost some of its identity as a reflection of life through the eyes and heart of faith. When spirituality began to lose its scriptural and theological foundations, it tended to become more private and subjective. During the twentieth century, there has been a growing synthesis between theology and spirituality.

Laity

Within the Catholic community, spirituality has been more linked with the clergy and members of religious congregations. The monastic tradition of spirituality implied that those who were serious about following Christ entered some form of religious life or the priesthood. Lay people had to do their best 'in the world'. Being a lay person was a kind of lesser option for disciples of Christ. There were many devotions such as Benediction, First Friday, the Mass, the Rosary and groups for lay people in parish life, such as Holy Name and Sacred Heart sodalities and the Legion of Mary. Lay people were encouraged to find their vocation in the home and the workplace.

Since Vatican II, there has been a recovery of the primal tradition of discipleship for all who are baptised. The call to holiness is for everybody, not just for those who are specially consecrated to God in an official Church group. Baptism is an initiation into the Christian community to share the gifts of grace. The laity's special role is to transform society with Kingdom values. Every Christian is challenged to be open to the Lord and to be a prophetic voice wherever she is.

The family is a kind of hearth for spirituality. It has the possibility to be a domestic church. Increased emphasis on family spirituality is helping family members to see the opportunities for grace within the ordinary interactions of everyday family life. Parents are the first teachers of the spiritual life. By their example they model religious values and rituals. As more married people assume leadership in the Church by holding administrative positions and in writing and speaking, spirituality of family and married life is gradually becoming more integrated into the mainstream of spiritual writings. Perhaps there is still some distance to go before a truly feminine lay spirituality is developed to balance the dominance of male celibate writings on the spiritual life.

Between 1950 and 1980 the composition of the teaching staffs of Catholic schools changed rapidly from religious to lay personnel. Although the overall transition went smoothly enough, many lay teachers were left without access to formation in spirituality. Resources for spiritual life development, in the form of retreats, conferences, spiritual directors, tapes, books, are much more accessible to priests and religious today. Administrators of Catholic schools have become more aware of the problem. Through such responses as the Colloquium, retreat days and formation courses, some teachers are being assisted. However I still discover many school staffs who have had little in-service opportunity to reflect on spirituality.

The secular values which pervade all aspects of western culture erode a Christian vision of humankind. Many parishes have lost their vitality as sources of religious socialisation. In such a materialistic climate, the nurturing of teacher spirituality cannot be left to chance. Each diocese or co-ordinating group should examine its priorities and evaluate how much attention is being devoted to the spiritual development of its teachers.

Ministry

Recently there has been a great upsurge of interest in an understanding of ministry and its expression in teaching. One of the special ministries named by Paul in his letter to the Corinthians is the ministry of teaching (1 Co 12:8). Teaching is a service to the community for instruction in the Christian way. The view of teaching as ministry offers many insights into a teacher's spirituality. Through the ministry of teaching, Christian educators share in the mission of Jesus as 'the finger of God', indicating a way of salvation.

Climate

Many teachers are searching for affirmation and support in their spiritual life. Spiritual development would be encouraged in a climate of joy and enthusiasm with a sensitive regard to religious freedoms and life situations. Heavy-handed moralising is counterproductive as well as being an affront to human dignity. The language used at conferences should be intelligible for teachers and the models of spirituality appropriate for lay people within a family context.

In this chapter, I have indicated some of the factors which have stimulated such an interest in spirituality for teachers. Our civilisation is confronted with serious threats to its well-being. A new consciousness of the environment is a reaction against ravages to the earth caused by pollution and nuclear installations. The emergence of many small groups – scripture prayer groups, Marriage Encounter, Crossroads, Antioch, Cursillo, Focalare, justice groups – is a sign of the dynamism of the Spirit. Teachers involved in Christian education recognise that the cultural environment of education is materialistic and no longer Christian. They also recognise that the new impetus for spirituality is an exciting invitation to grow more deeply into religious faith.

REFLECTION

1. Why is there such a need for a teacher to develop spirituality?

2. In what ways do you feel supported (or not supported) in your spiritual life?

3. Consider the many teachers who have influenced your life. Which teachers impressed you? What quality did these teachers possess which touched your life?

4. Have you participated in a prayer group or parish renewal group? In what ways does this group assist your spiritual life?

5. Draw circles to represent some 'stepping stones', or special times in your spiritual life.

Name each of the 'stepping stones' on your spiritual journey.

SCRIPTURE

Jeremiah 1:4-9
> The word of Yahweh was addressed to me, saying,
> 'Before I formed you in the womb I knew you;
> before you came to birth I consecrated you;
> I have appointed you as prophet to the nations.'
> I said, 'Ah, Lord Yahweh; look, I do not know how to speak: I am a child!'
> But Yahweh replied,.
> 'Do not say, "I am a child".
> Go now to those to whom I send you
> and say whatever I command you.
> Do not be afraid of them,
> for I am with you to protect you –
> it is Yahweh who speaks!'

Luke 6:47-49
> Jesus said, 'Everyone who comes to me and listens to my words and acts on them – I will show you what he is like. He is like the man who when he built his house dug, and dug deep, and laid the foundations on rock; when the river was in flood it bore down on that house but could not shake it, it was so well built. But the one who listens and does nothing is like the man who built his house on soil, with no foundations: as soon as the river bore down on it, it collapsed; and what a ruin that house became!'

Luke 18:15-17
> People even brought little children to him, for him to touch them; but when the disciples saw this they turned them away. But Jesus called the children to him and said, 'Let the children come to me, and do not stop them; for it is to such as these that the kingdom of God belongs. I tell you solemnly, anyone who does not welcome the kingdom of God like a little child will never enter it.'

1 Corinthians 12:4-11
> There is a variety of gifts but always the same Spirit; there are all sorts of service to be done, but always to the same Lord; working in all sorts of different ways in different people, it is the same God who is working in all of them. The particular way in which the Spirit is given to each person is for a good purpose. One may have the gift of preaching with wisdom given him by the Spirit; another may have the gift of preaching instruction given him by the same Spirit; and another the gift of faith given by the same Spirit, another again the gift of healing, through this one Spirit; one, the power of miracles; another, prophecy, another the gift of recognising spirits; another the gift of tongues and another the ability to interpret them. All these are the work of one and the same Spirit, who distributes different gifts to different people just as he chooses.

3

THE HERITAGE OF SPIRITUALITY

In order to appreciate a spirituality for teachers, we might reflect on the extraordinary diversity of spiritual styles and devotions throughout the history of Christianity. In imagination, we may travel from the brave martyrs facing death in Rome, to the hermits of Egypt, to the chanting monks of monasteries in the Middle Ages, to the Salvation Army workers in London's East End, to the Christian communities in Senegal. In every age and society, there have been different ways by which people have responded to the invitation of Jesus: 'Follow me' (Lk 6:28). When teachers are exploring their own spiritual paths, they may draw inspiration and wisdom from the rich heritage of two thousand years of Christian spirituality. Then, like the householder of Matthew's gospel: 'who brings out from his storeroom things both old and new' (Mt 13:52), teachers may incorporate traditional forms of spirituality into their own religious aspirations.

Christian spirituality is like a tapestry with many colours. The two thousand years of the Christian story tell of the millions of women and men of many cultures and eras who have sought an experience of God according to their levels of consciousness in that era. Christian people have understood their faith and prayer in various cultural forms, styles and symbols. Devotional expressions in one era may be inappropriate for a later age or different culture. There are certain common elements in Christian spirituality, such as God's loving concern for us, the redemptive grace of Christ, the need for prayer, but the explicit forms of today's spirituality may not be tomorrow's.

The early Church

Jesus gathered together a group of disciples as a community. The community of disciples was sent to announce the new reign of God: 'And as you go, proclaim that the kingdom of heaven is close at hand' (Mt 10:7). The Holy Spirit, the Paraclete or Advocate, was the energising power. 'While Peter was still speaking the Holy Spirit came down on all the listeners' (Ac 10:44). The way of discipleship was for all followers of Christ, not just for any religious elite. Any notion that some people were called to holiness and others were not, is quite alien to the New Testament account of spirituality. Vocational distinctions are largely absent from its pages.

With the advent of the persecutions, the heroes and heroines of the Church were the martyrs. These brave people represented the climax of what it means to be a Christian – that is, a willingness to die for Christ. After the persecution era had ended in the fourth century, opportunities for martyrdom were rare, except in certain areas. Fleeing from the world to a hermitage or refuge became the new form of physical martyrdom. Communities of monks emerged from these refuges and the monastic movement was born. By the sixth century, monasteries were well established, especially from the tradition of Benedict. The monastic ideal became the most esteemed expression of spirituality.

Although early monasticism was essentially a lay movement, it was based on a 'flight from the world' view. The world was perceived as evil – not a place where one might live the spiritual life. The monasteries flourished in the places where Europe was being Christianised and their influence went far beyond the monastery walls. Many people lived close to the monasteries and although they were not actually monks, their way of life and their spirituality were closely modelled on monastic spirituality.

The rise of a dualistic view of humankind tended to

denigrate the essential wholeness of a person. The philosophies of Gnosticism, Stoicism, Neoplatonism and Manichaeism perceived the good principle of the soul imprisoned in the material evil of the body. Writers such as Origen, Basil, John Cassian, Augustine and Pseudo-Dionysius taught about the spiritual life from a dualistic framework. One consequence of this dualistic approach was a kind of two-tiered understanding of spirituality. In this view those who had renounced the 'flesh' to live in a monastery had chosen a 'higher' form of spirituality than those who stayed in the world. The latter were spiritual second-class citizens. This dualism had the effect of reducing the laity to a position of inferiority in the Church from which they are only now emerging. It also had a very negative attitude towards sexuality and marriage.

Another influence was the growing institutional forms in the Church. By the Middle Ages the clerical system had subsumed all ministries under the ministry of ordination. The disappearance of a pluralism of ministries, so characteristic of life in the early Church, tended to emphasise an office approach to spirituality. This approach suggested that one was serious about the spiritual life if one entered into some office of the Church, e.g. by becoming a priest or religious.

Benedictine spirituality has been very significant in the story of Christian spirituality. Benedict (480-547) stressed the value of work and its noble role in human life. The Benedictine view was in sharp contrast with the prevailing perception of work as degrading and more worthy of the lowest classes in society.

The Middle Ages
During the Middle Ages, religious orders such as the Franciscans, Carmelites, Dominicans and Augustinians were founded and each group has left a rich heritage to the many spiritual paths. These orders, especially the

Franciscans, sought to touch the lives of ordinary people. During the Middle Ages, devotions flourished. Devotion to the Blessed Eucharist, the Heart of Jesus, Mary and the saints, together with fasting, discipline, statues and processions were widespread expressions of a vital spiritual life.

This era is also a period of mysticism. Meister Eckhart and the Rhineland mystics were very influential. Thomas à Kempis' *Imitation of Christ* reflected much of the thinking of the fourteenth century. *The Cloud of Unknowing* by an anonymous English author was written at this time and is still a classic in spirituality. It stressed that flight from the world to contemplation was the desired way to holiness. During the fourteenth and fifteenth centuries, confraternities and guilds engaged in spiritual formation of their members through prayer and devotional practices.

1500-1900

The Reformation was a time of intense spiritual activity. One of the great figures of Christian spirituality, Ignatius of Loyola, sought to integrate the apostolate and contemplation. Ignatius saw good in the world as well as evil. His methods for discernment of spirits were taught to help people find paths to God through their work.

Ignatian spirituality, which stresses a personal relationship with Christ, was fostered by the Jesuit congregation which Ignatius founded, and has been a major influence on spiritual writings and practices in the Christian community since the sixteenth century. Three other outstanding people at this time were Teresa of Avila (d. 1582), John of the Cross (d. 1591) and Martin Luther (d. 1546). Teresa and John wrote on the mystic way of union with God's love through prayer and contemplation. Luther emphasised the individual's approach to God through scripture reading and meditation.

A person who did much for lay spirituality was Francis

de Sales (d. 1622). His *Introduction to the Devout Life* was written for those 'who have to live in the world and who, according to their state, to all outward appearance have to live an ordinary life'. Francis and others, such as Alphonsus Ligouri and Jean Jacques Olier, sought to combat the negative influences of Jansenism. Jansenism portrayed human nature in gloomy terms. Another extreme view which affected thinking on the spiritual life was Quietism, which proposed that human nature was powerless to engage in the spiritual life. Our role was passive. God's grace was the force in spirituality.

The rise of the missionary congregations during the nineteenth century disseminated French and Irish traditions of spirituality throughout the world. Congregations like the Sisters of Mercy, the Presentation Sisters, the Franciscan and Brigidine Sisters, and the Sisters of St Joseph carried a simple piety to the homes of millions of Catholics through the apostolate of Catholic schools, parishes and hospitals. Men's congregations like the Marists, the De La Salle and Christian Brothers, the Jesuits, the Missionaries of the Sacred Heart, the Dominicans, Franciscans, Vincentians and Carmelites, touched the lives of many by their ministry in schools, parishes and retreat centres. The London Missionary Society was a major force in evangelical mission spirituality. Colonel Booth's Salvation Army workers expressed in a dramatic way the spirituality of service to Christ's poor.

John Wesley (1703-91) emphasised that the preaching of the gospel would lead to conversion. He influenced many generations of preachers with his commitment to the poor who had become victims of vast social changes brought about by the rising industrialisation of England.

The twentieth century

The twentieth century has been remarkable in the vitality and diversity of its spiritual movements. The threats to spiritual values from national and international violence, world wars, secularism, marxism and capitalism, have provoked people to search for God with a new urgency. The long shadows of ecological destruction and nuclear armaments have stimulated new quests for appreciating the value of men and women made in the image of God living on this earth. By the middle of the century, some definite trends in spirituality were appearing.

Spirituality:

- became more holistic, concerned with the whole person, not simply with 'the soul';
- was more communal and liturgically orientated. It was less individualistic;
- emphasised that Baptism was the starting point of the spiritual life for all people, religious, clerical and lay;
- needed to find expression in service to restore justice in the world;
- was more ecumenical in wishing to incorporate the wisdom of east and west, including the great religious heritage of religions such as Buddhism, Hinduism, Islam and Judaism;
- was often developed within the context of small groups;
- was ecclesial, with a sense of church as Christian community, sharing prayer and committed to Kingdom action;
- was concerned about earth consciousness and ecology, linking us to the whole of the cosmos;
- was situated within the context of ordinary life, the family, the workplace.

Two other features of latter twentieth-century spirituality were the contribution of the charismatic movement in stressing the role of the Holy Spirit in the spiritual life and, more recently, the emergence of creation spirituality. Contemporary spirituality has been enhanced by writers like Karl Rahner, Evelyn Underhill, C.S. Lewis, Thomas Merton, Simone Weil, Martin Buber, William Johnston and Henri Nouwen.

Looking back over the story of Christian spirituality we notice that the early equality in spirituality changed to an emphasis on monasteries with a consequent neglect of lay spirituality. Vatican II has reaffirmed the vocation of all baptised people as disciples. Spirituality today is much more incarnational, concerned with finding the Lord in the everyday, ordinary actions of life, and not in fleeing to some remote refuge. Spirituality is less organised and very vital. It is relational and involved with the world situation.

REFLECTION

1. Was your spiritual life influenced by any religious congregation? In what ways?

2. Identify some movements in the spirituality that you experience or observe in your parish, school or neighbourhood.

3. What things would help you now, as you consider the development of your spirituality? What kind of support would people appreciate on their spiritual journey?

4. Draw a time line and map some main movements in the story of Christian spirituality.

5. What do you understand by 'lay' spirituality?

Paths and Stories

SCRIPTURE

John 14:1-4
    Jesus said,
    'Do not let your hearts be troubled.
    Trust in God still, and trust in me.
    There are many rooms in my Father's house;
    if there were not, I should have told you.
    I am going now to prepare a place for you,
    and after I have gone and prepared you a place,
    I shall return to take you with me;
    so that where I am
    you may be too.
    You know the way to the place where I am going.'

Genesis 12:1-3
    Yahweh said to Abram, 'Leave your country, your family and your Father's house, for the land I will show you. I will make you a great nation; I will bless you and make your name so famous that it will be used as a blessing.
      'I will bless those who bless you;
      I will curse those who slight you.
      All the tribes of the earth
      shall bless themselves by you.'

1 Peter 4:7-11
    Everything will soon come to an end, so, to pray better, keep a calm and sober mind. Above all, never let your love for each other grow insincere, since love covers over many a sin. Welcome each other into your houses without grumbling. Each one of you has received a special grace, so, like good stewards responsible for all these different graces of God, put yourselves at the service of others. If you are a speaker, speak in words which seem to come from God; if you are helper, help as though every action was done at God's orders; so that in

The heritage of spirituality

everything God may receive the glory, through Jesus Christ, since to him alone belong all glory and power for ever and ever. Amen.

Leviticus 26:3-13

If you live according to my laws, if you keep my commandments and put them into practice, I will give you the rain you need at the right time; the earth shall give its produce and the trees of the countryside their fruits; you shall thresh until vintage time and gather grapes until sowing time. You shall eat your fill of bread and live secure in your land.

4

JESUS THE TEACHER

We may gain insights into the spirituality of a teacher by observing Jesus as teacher, a model for Christian teachers.

Jesus is addressed as 'teacher'. Nicodemus comes by night and says to Jesus: 'Rabbi, we know you are a teacher who comes from God' (Jn 3:2). Jesus is specifically called 'rabbi' on a number of occasions (Mk 11:21, Mk 9:5). The term implied that Jesus was a religious teacher and he spoke with authority. Jesus as rabbi would be a familiar figure with the people of first-century Palestine. Rabbis gathered disciples and travelled about the country, expounding the Law. The place of teaching was often in the synagogue (Mt 4:23; Mk 6:2), but rabbis also taught in the market place or in the countryside wherever the crowds would gather.

Jesus did not simply expound the Law as did the other rabbis. He taught his own doctrines announcing that the Kingdom of God had arrived. He taught on his own authority and as one sent by God (Jn 7:16). In parables he sought to reveal the wondrous mystery of God's gracious love and call to reconciliation.

Jesus emphasised that the Torah (the Way of Life) was to be lived and respected. He criticised the scribes for studying the Law and yet not being able to convey its spirit of compassion. His teaching did not follow the tradition of the scholars who so often reduced the study of the Law to an arid dissection of legal statements.

Jesus made a great impact on his listeners: '... his teaching made a deep impression on the people because he taught them with authority, and not like their own scribes' (Mt 7:28-29).

Jesus the teacher

The context of Jesus as teacher is set in the Hebrew tradition of wisdom. The search for wisdom is the endeavour to discover the right path. Wisdom is a gift of Yahweh: 'Yahweh himself is giver of wisdom, from his mouth issue knowledge and discernment... he stands guard over the paths of justice, he keeps watch on the way of his devoted ones. Then you will understand what virtue is, justice and fair dealing, all paths that lead to happiness (Pr 2:6, 8-9).

The wise person is one who reflects on God's creation with a sense of awe in its majesty and mystery: 'The spirit of the Lord, indeed, fills the whole world, and that which holds all things together knows every word that is said' (Ws 1:7).

The teacher as sage or wise person discerns the true way to God and happiness. She or he rejects the many false gods which seek to seduce the teacher and students from truth. The wise person is encouraged to pursue the quest for wisdom:

Seek Yahweh while he is still to be found,
call to him while he is still near (Is 55:6).

The invitation to wisdom is offered by a God who asks:

Oh, come to the water all you who are thirsty;
though you have no money, come!
Buy corn without money, and eat,
and, at no cost, wine and milk.
Why spend money on what is not bread,
your wages on what fails to satisfy?
Listen, listen to me, and you will have good things to eat
and rich foods to enjoy.
Pay attention, come to me;
listen, and your soul will live (Is 55:1-3).

The people who listened to Jesus recognised his wisdom.

Paths and Stories

Even at the age of twelve, Jesus astounded the doctors of the Law: 'and all those who heard him were astounded at his intelligence and his replies' (Lk 2:46). Wisdom had come to the Temple. The wisdom of Jesus flowed from his relationship with his Father:

> Father, may they be one in us,
> as you are in me and I am in you (Jn 17:21).

Jesus identified with God's wisdom. As teacher he revealed the way of happiness: 'Seeing the crowds Jesus went up the hill. There he sat down and was joined by his disciples. Then he began to speak. This is what he taught them:

> How happy are the poor in spirit;
> theirs is the kingdom of heaven (Mt 5:3).

Paul saw Christ as wisdom: 'here are we preaching a crucified Christ.. a Christ who is the power and wisdom of God' (1 Co 1:25). The Christian community thus received from Israel's wisdom literature an appreciation of Jesus as the very epitome of wisdom, the wise teacher.

Features of Jesus the teacher
The gospel profile of Jesus the teacher offers the following characteristics about the style of Jesus as teacher:

1. Story-teller
Jesus told stories to jolt the conventional thinking of his listeners. The Kingdom of God was such a radical dream for new possibilities of relating to each other and Abba, that it required the surprise of a parable story to tease our imaginations. Parables were like magic carpets to take us beyond our stereotyped boundaries. The symbols of story cannot be exhausted, they lead us to other places where we can re-examine our values and actions in the light of the

Jesus the teacher

dawning of the Kingdom. Somehow, the openings 'Once upon a time...', or 'The Kingdom of God is like...' suggest another realm of thinking about someone or something. Matthew records that 'The people all stood on the beach, and he told them many things in parables' (Mt 13:3). As a story-teller Jesus used everyday accounts of travellers being ambushed, shepherds, servants, labourers in the field, bakers and sleepy wedding attendants.

2. Healer

Jesus healed as he taught. His teaching was a liberation of the spirit. The healing miracles symbolised this liberation. In the missioning of the Twelve, Mark's gospel reports the first apostles being sent on mission: 'So they set off to preach repentance; and they cast out many devils, and anointed many sick people with oil and cured them' (Mk 6:13). Jesus healed the lame, the blind, lepers and those with paralysis, and he exorcised demons (Mk 5:1-20). People who were given sight and freedom from possession by spirits, who were restored to wholesome bodies from leprosy, represented and symbolised the new reconciliation of the reign of God. Jesus as teacher accompanied his oral teaching by a presence which invited his listeners to share the *shalom* of God's wish for restoration.

3. Challenge

Jesus issued challenges to his followers and to the crowds. Discipleship is certainly not for the fainthearted. Jesus confronted people. The rich young man was asked to sell his possessions (Lk 18:18-23); the Syro-Phoenician woman was addressed in a provocative way (Mk 7:27); the woman at the well was reminded about her promiscuity (Jn 24:18); the followers on the lakeside were bewildered after hearing about the bread from heaven (Jn 6:60). In teaching, he dared them to think beyond their limited boundaries. Some listeners were moved by the challenge to change their ways, e.g. Zacchaeus (Lk 19:1-10); others were stirred to vengeful fury (Mk 3:6: 'The Pharisees went out.. discussing how to destroy him'). The teachings of Jesus were directed to the heart, not simply to the intellect, and thus the response was sometimes violent when people felt threatened.

4. Reflection

Jesus is recorded as beginning his day in prayer. 'In the morning, long before dawn, he got up and left the house, and went off to a lonely place and prayed there' (Mk 1:35-36). His intimacy with his Father was strengthened by long hours of contemplation: 'Everything has been entrusted to me by my Father; and no one knows who the Son is except the Father, and who the Father is except the Son' (Lk 10:22). The desert was the symbol of the place where one met God, a kind of stark, no-hiding place from God and oneself. Before Jesus began his teaching, he experienced a struggle with options for his path to ministry. Jesus 'was led by the Spirit through the wilderness' (Lk 4:1). Jesus, the wise teacher, sought and discovered wisdom through reflection on the Father's love. In the book of Proverbs we read: 'Let the wise listen and he will learn yet more, and the man of discernment will acquire the art of guidance' (Pr 1:5). Jesus, indeed a man of discernment, was a listener to people's hearts. In the Emmaus story (Lk 24:13-35), Jesus asked the two downcast disciples what was troubling them. Before he offered an explanation of the passion, he drew out their stories. Happy, said Jesus are 'those who hear the word of God and keep it' (Lk 11:28).

5. Empowering

As a teacher, Jesus was concerned that the gifts of others should be realised. His power was to empower his listeners to experience the liberation of daughters and sons of God. The poor man living among the tombs in Gerasene

(Mk 5:1-20) is almost a symbol of the ultimate in hopelessness. Yet this moving story of exorcism ends with this man being empowered to become a missionary to his people: 'Go home to your people and tell them all that the Lord in his mercy has done for you' (Mk 5:19). The woman taken in adultery (Jn 8:3-11) is sent away in peace. Jesus wished his teaching to be freeing in affirmation and a formula for authentic human values.

> If you make my word your home
> you will indeed be my disciples,
> you will learn the truth
> and the truth will make you free (Jn 8:31-32).

6. Love and Compassion
Ultimately the criterion for discipleship is love. A Christian teacher faces the real test of loving her or his students. There can be no quibbling or dodging this command from Jesus the teacher:

> This is my commandment:
> love one another,
> as I have loved you (Jn 15:12).

The missioning of the disciples by Jesus is stated as revelation of God's love in Jesus:

> As you sent me into the world,
> I have sent them into the world,
> ... so that the world will realise it was you who sent me
> and that I have loved them as much as you love me
> (Jn 17:18-23).

The gentleness of Jesus' love is evident when he witnesses their helplessness and poverty: 'And when he saw the crowds he felt sorry for them because they were harassed and dejected, like sheep without a shepherd'

(Mt 9:36). The sight of the leper, the widow of Nain, the widow with her mite, the sinful woman, moved the heart of Jesus to reach out and express his solidarity and compassion. His compassion expressed the spirit of his teaching.

7. Authority

Jesus taught with authority arising from the conviction of his call by the Father. During the Baptism of Jesus, the Spirit descended upon him and a voice from heaven said, 'You are my Son, the Beloved; my favour rests on you' (Mk 1:11). Luke describes the mission of Jesus thus: 'He went down to Capernaum, a town in Galilee, and taught them on the sabbath. And his teaching made a deep impression on them because he spoke with authority' (Lk 4:31-32). A constant theme in the teaching of Jesus was one of being sent by the Father and in turn he sends forth the disciples. His utter conviction of the Kingdom message and personal witness to Kingdom values gave an urgency and authority to his teaching.

8. Failure

As a teacher, Jesus suffered the pain of rejection and indifference. One of the most poignant scenes of the gospel is the lonely figure of Jesus weeping over the failure of Jerusalem to listen: 'How often have I longed to gather your children as a hen gathers her chicks under her wings, and you refused! So be it!' (Mt 23:37). It is hard for a teacher to feel a lack of appreciation or acceptance. Jesus was declared insane by his relatives in Nazareth (Mk 3:21). One of his twelve sold him for thirty pieces of silver and the leaders sought to kill him. Yet, mysteriously, the anguish of the suffering Servant Jesus is not sterile. It transforms to new life:

> Unless a wheat grain falls on the ground and dies,
> it remains only a single grain;

but if it dies,
it yields a rich harvest (Jn 12:24).

Suffering is a mirror to show our mortality, our limits. The trauma of Jesus carried him to a new depth of submission. He cried out: 'Father, into your hands I commit my Spirit' (Lk 23:46). The last breath of Jesus was the first breath of the Spirit for the new age.

9. Service

Jesus adopted a radical stance towards power and status. His followers were stunned to be confronted with the paradox of being told they must be servants: 'Anyone who wants to be great among you must be your servant, and anyone who wants to be first among you must be your slave, just as the Son of Man came not to be served but to serve' (Mt 20:26-28). According to Jesus, to be a teacher is to accept that teaching is service. It is a ministry of self-giving, not in the sense of being a doormat for people to trample upon, but using power to set people free through loving service.

10. Community

As soon as Jesus commenced teaching, he gathered around him a community of disciples (Mk 1:14-20). Christian teaching is situated firmly within the community which should be supportive of the teacher. The Kingdom teacher is called to a new quality of relationships which transcends the narrow boundaries set by stereotypes and racism. The presence of Jesus is discovered in the gathering of the community: 'For where two or three meet in my name, I shall be there with them' (Mt 18:20). Jesus attached great importance to the community in his teaching style. The community clarified ideas, celebrated together, experienced conflict, grew in commitment to the ideals of the Kingdom of God. After the death of Jesus, the Holy Spirit inspired the early Christian community to spread the teachings of Jesus.

11. Vocation

The story of the Baptism of Jesus (see Mk 1:9-11) describes his calling to mission. Each of the images in the story suggests a vocation theme:

'No sooner had he come up out of the water'	– coming out of water is a consciousness of taking a new step in life.
'he saw the heavens torn apart'	– a new era is dawning with the teaching of Jesus.
'and the Spirit, like a dove, descending on him'	– Jesus is being missioned by the Spirit to create new life in the world.
'and the voice came from heaven, "You are my son, the Beloved: my favour rests on you"'	– Jesus is the Son of God, chosen and blessed by God.

During his life, Jesus was very conscious of his vocation to be a teacher sent by God:

> When you have lifted up the Son of Man,
> then you will know that I am He
> and that I do nothing of myself;
> what the Father has taught me
> is what I preach;
> he who sent me is with me (Jn 8:28-29).

In the concluding section of the Last Discourse, Jesus prays that his mission will be continued through his disciples:

I have glorified you on earth
and finished the work
that you gave me to do...
I have made your name known
to the men you took from the world to give me.
As you sent me into the world,
I have sent them into the world,
and for their sake I consecrate myself
so that they too may be consecrated in truth'.
(Jn 17:4,6,18)

Jesus was driven by the utter conviction of his vocation to teach. All kinds of obstacles in the form of family rejection, poverty of circumstances, fickleness of followers, death threats, bitter opposition from the religious authorities, did not and could not deter Jesus from pursuing the path he had chosen to preach the Good News of the Kingdom of God.

I have briefly described in this chapter some of the features of Jesus as teacher. By reflecting on Jesus the teacher, Christian teachers may evaluate their own styles and models of how they teach. Although the era of first-century Palestine and its culture have long faded into history, the themes in the story of Jesus as teacher are as relevant today as they were two thousand years ago.

Paths and Stories

REFLECTION

1. Here are some features of Jesus as teacher. Search for an appropriate gospel story or passage which illustrates this feature and find an application in your style of teaching.

Jesus as teacher

Feature	Scripture passage	Teaching application
Story-teller	Matthew 13:24-30 Weeds and wheat	Make a collection of stories for the children
Servant		
Healer		
Suffering one		
Community builder		

2. What quality of Jesus the Teacher impresses you most?

3. What comparisons might be made between the cultural and religious context of the time of Jesus and your present teaching cultural situation?

4. If Jesus was teaching today, where would he teach? To whom?

   What would his style of teaching be?

SCRIPTURE

Matthew 13:53-58

When Jesus had finished these parables he left the district; and, coming to his home town, he taught the people in their synagogue in such a way that they were astonished and said, 'Where did the man get this wisdom and these miraculous powers? This is the carpenter's son, surely? Is not his mother the woman called Mary, and his brothers James and Joseph and Simon and Jude? His sisters, too, are they not all here with us? So where did the man get it all?' And they would not accept him. But Jesus said to them, 'A prophet is only despised in his own country and in his own house', and he did not work many miracles there because of their lack of faith.

John 8:12

Jesus said:
'I am the light of the world;
anyone who follows me will not be walking in the dark;
he will have the light of life.'

Matthew 5:21-24

Jesus said, 'You have learnt how it was said to our ancestors: You must not kill; and if anyone does kill he must answer for it before the court. But I say this to you: anyone who is angry with his brother will answer for it before the court; if a man calls his brother "fool" he will answer for it before the Sanhedrin; and if a man calls him "Renegade" he will answer for it in hell fire. So then, if you are bringing your offering to the altar and there remember that your brother has something against you, leave your offering there before the altar; go and be reconciled with your brother first, and then come back and present your offering.'

Paths and Stories

Matthew 10:1-10

Jesus summoned his twelve disciples, and gave them authority over unclean spirits with power to cast them out and to cure all kinds of diseases and sickness.

These are the names of the twelve apostles: first, Simon who is called Peter, and his brother Andrew; James the son of Zebedee, and his brother John; Philip and Bartholomew; Thomas, and Matthew the tax collector; James the son of Alphaeus, and Thaddaeus; Simon the Zealot and Judas Iscariot, the one who was to betray him. These twelve Jesus sent out, instructing them as follows:

'Do not turn your steps to pagan territory, and do not enter any Samaritan town; go rather to the lost sheep of the House of Israel. And as you go, proclaim that the kingdom of heaven is close at hand. Cure the sick, raise the dead, cleanse the lepers, cast out devils. You received without charge, give without charge. Provide yourselves with no gold or silver, not even with a few coppers for your purses, with no haversack for the journey or spare tunic or footwear or a staff, for the workman deserves his keep.'

5

THE TEACHER AS A CREATION PERSON

One of the most stimulating courses I have taken as a student at university was taught by Maria Harris in Boston. The course was entitled 'Aesthetics and Religious Education'. The classes were exciting and it was with a sense of anticipation that I entered the class each week. I recall dressing as a clown and wandering about some streets doing clowning. The experience left a vivid impression on me. I felt that another dimension of being a human person had been revealed to me, enabling me to see the world from another perspective. A teacher's role is to be a life or creation person, enabling students to see the world from the perspective of imagination.

A teacher's spirituality is a generative one, it is concerned with life, life-giving and life-receiving. Leading students to a fullness of life is a goal of a Christian teacher. Jesus as life-giver expresses this yearning:

> Let anyone who is thirsty come to me!
> Let anyone who believes in me come and drink! (Jn 7:38).

or again:

> I have come
> so that they may have life
> and have it to the full (Jn 10:10).

His beautiful image of bread is an evocative symbol of life:

> I am the bread of life (Jn 6:48).

Ecclesiasticus presents us with the respect of choice in the way we seek life:

> He has set fire and water before you;
> put out your hand to whichever you prefer.
> A human being has life and death before him;
> whichever he prefers will be given him' (Si 15:16-17).

All of us in school days or as adults have experienced teachers who taught as life people. There was something in their enthusiasm, their creativity or thoroughness which gave us a sense of accomplishment, of challenge and acquisition of knowledge. Perhaps too, we remember teachers who dulled us into boredom or oppressed us by their manipulative teaching. A Christian teacher is concerned with continuing the creative energy of God in the world. This kind of person needs to be committed to a spirituality of creation.

What is spirituality of creation?

Story
One feature of creation spirituality is a sense of story in a teacher's life. She is also able to see her life as an unfolding of events, which are happy or sad or paradoxical. The 'once upon a time' theme recalls the journey with its hills, paths, valleys and passages to new places in our life. The story of our life goes on, it is always being told, it is a never-ending story.

Our own life story is greatly enriched if we pass over to other people's stories, not in judgment, but in compassion. We can then return to our own story with new insights. We can marvel at how the mysterious Lord of the journeys has been with us on the way. Through prayer and reflection, we may also enter the story of God. God is always asking us to be incorporated into the Great Story which has the refrain,

'I love you, come and live happily for ever with me'.

To remember our story is an invitation to faith. In remembering our story, we stand with the memories of many caring and loving people. We remember too the pain of rejection and hurts which constitute many pages of our biography. Remembering is a time of grace if we try to say 'yes' to its mystery. Being in touch with our stories is an imperative for teachers because their vocations lead them to enter so many stories of their students. If a teacher renounces her story, the pain festers and it may be projected onto vulnerable students who are confused by the angers and aggressions arising from an unattended teacher's story.

Healing the life story is a critical aspect of a teacher's spirituality.

Blessing
Another aspect of creation spirituality is the celebration of life as a gift. Everything we have is gift. This celebration is pervaded by a sense of *berakah* or blessings.

In consumer oriented societies it is easy to become locked into a mind-set which is always seeking something we don't have. In creation spirituality, we celebrate what we have, every little thing – our lives, our health, our bodies, our home, our families, our country, our gifts. Teachers can be very demanding people. Professionally they have to be systematic in the pursuit of excellence. Teachers are fairly critical in the way they relate. It is so easy to take others for granted, to become casual about the mystery of each person. Sometimes, it might be helpful for a teacher to allow his eyes to move around a classroom or adult gathering, consciously recalling the names of the people in the class, becoming aware of their faces, their gifts, their expressions, being aware that behind each face there is some sacred story. These people are loved by God. Such a belief is a sheer act of faith with some class groups! Some distancing from or perspective on our students often helps to develop a sense of appreciation. Teachers may develop an atmosphere of blessing by such activities as: saying grace before meals, holding blessing services with the class, admiring a waterfall or a sunset, marvelling at a computer, giving thanks for special events in life, stroking a cat. All these are moments of the *berakah*. When we learn to celebrate the marvels of life, we become wonder people. By being attuned to wonder, we meet the God of surprises in the most unexpected places. The biblical refrain 'I will bless you...' (Gn 12:2) should be an echo in the spirituality of a teacher. The ultimate inspiration for *berakah* spirituality is surely the awareness of being loved unconditionally by God:

> We ourselves have known and put our faith in
> God's love towards ourselves.
> God is love
> and anyone who lives in love lives in God,
> and God lives in him (1 Jn 4:16).

Sabbath

The pressurised routine of teaching may result in a teacher feeling drained of energy. Each day is like walking a treadmill of professional and family demands. Teachers sometimes have the sense of doing a giant juggling act, throwing up and catching the many balls of family responsibilities, preparation of lessons, attendance at school functions, social and church gatherings. Burn-out and over-tiredness are deadly threats to creation spirituality.

For a teacher to be a creation person, he must allow space and time for himself. Professional and family demands need to be balanced. The sabbath was originated by Yahweh so that the work of creation could be continued through rest. Recreation means to 're-create'. The sabbath moves us from 'chronos' time of clocks and schedules, to 'kairos' time of opportunities for grace. Sabbath time is wasting time, of allowing time to come to us, rather than controlling and organising time. A teacher might well ask how he experiences the sabbath. In what ways is the energy of Spirit given space to breathe into his life?

The Book of Kings has a powerful story about discovering God's presence in the gentle breeze. The breeze is an image of sabbath space enabling us to encounter God:

> Then [Elijah] was told, 'Go out and stand on the mountain before Yahweh.' Then Yahweh himself went by. There came a mighty wind so strong it tore the mountains and shattered the rocks before Yahweh. But Yahweh was not in the wind. After the wind came an earthquake. After the earthquake came a fire. But Yahweh was not in the fire. And after the fire there came the sound of a gentle breeze (1 K 19:11-13).

There are many earthquakes, fires and mighty winds in teaching, stressful class behaviour problems, sense of failure, staff tensions, late night preparations, juggling family and teaching commitments. Teachers need regular sabbath gentle breezes to find Yahweh and relax.

The sabbath enables a teacher to gain a perspective in faith on what is happening. The Spirit works in the hearts of students. Being a teacher involves much waiting for planted seeds to take root and bear fruit. The sabbath recalls how periods of gestation are necessary for growth. The sabbath is a memorial to the dwelling of God in the universe.

Earth consciousness

A key element in creation spirituality is earth consciousness. By earth consciousness we mean a reverence for the earth and an awareness of our connectedness to it. God made a covenant with us and the earth (Gn 9). We are part of earth. A teacher should strive to develop a religious sense of the land. Our affinity with the earth will help our students to have an appreciation that we are stewards, not dominators, of the land. Our land is being ravaged by pollution, erosion and irresponsible land use. Nuclear weapons threaten our very life existence. By raising earth consciousness, teachers share in the ongoing creative action of God in building the earth and the cosmos. There are many ways to integrate earth consciousness into a teacher's spirituality, such as: gardening, walking, camping, growing pot plants, surfing, visiting nature parks and learning to pause to marvel at the wonders of earth life.

Love
Love is the primal energising force in the world. Love brings forth new creations. It enables people to grow, to share, to reach out in confidence. Love has many faces. Love may touch, fondle, slap, hold, cry, celebrate and appreciate. To love one another we need to love ourselves. There are so many opportunities for love in a teacher's life. Teachers demonstrate their love of their students by fidelity to their welfare, by listening, and by respecting them. Perhaps love needs to be named, at least sometimes, but the students know if their teacher loves them. The effects of love are obvious. The media stereotype of love is often a packaged one to slot within the scheduled one-hour programme. A Christian love has its genesis in God's love for us in Jesus. In the first letter of John we read:

> My dear people,
> let us love one another
> since love comes from God
> and everyone who loves is begotten by God
> and knows God.
> Anyone who fails to love can never have known God,

because God is love.
God's love for us was revealed
when God sent into the world his only Son
so that we could have life through him;
this is the love I mean:
not our love for God,
but God's love for us when he sent his Son
to be the sacrifice that takes our sins away (1 Jn 4:7-11).

Because our love has so many conditions and limits, we might find it difficult to comprehend the wondrous love of God for us. Our human experiences in love, with its joys and hurts, make us cautious in loving. The implications of the revelation 'God is love' are mind-blowing for a teacher's spirituality. God is saying to us to take a faith leap into the mystery of God's love and to keep believing in its power, sometimes in spite of contrary evidence.

Sexuality
Through our sexuality we express love. Creation people rejoice in their sexuality. A life-giving teacher is one who celebrates being woman or man. She or he seeks to integrate the inner face of her or his sexuality.

Our outer face gives us our sexual identity but our inner face, the feminine for a man, the masculine for a woman, gives us the face of our unconscious sexuality. In a sense we are bisexual.

Sometimes sexuality has been regarded as a hindrance to the spiritual life. Yet sexuality is at the core of our humanity. A teacher's role is a relational one. He is involved with people by the very nature of being a teacher. There is a certain vulnerability in teaching. Teachers need to show that they can be touched by the other. However, if a teacher is too vulnerable he can be crushed by students and the school or parish system. The other extreme, i.e. being too aloof and remote, leaves students confused and frustrated by the apparent indifference of the teacher. A healthy sexuality enables a teacher to engage in intimacy. Intimacy occurs when we open ourselves to the gift of the other. Unless there is a mutual respect and love, the relationship becomes one-sided or manipulative.

The child image expresses the generativity of our sexuality. The Christ child of Bethlehem is the original symbol of the Incarnation. The injunction by Jesus, 'Unless you change and become like little children, you will never enter the Kingdom of heaven' (Mt 18:3) is an imperative for conversion to simplicity and imagination. The *metanoia* to the Christ child enables us to bring forth the child with us, the child of trust and creativity. A teacher who is a gospel child takes great interest in her students, she enjoys meeting them, prays for their welfare and celebrates with them. A 'little child' spirituality finds the Kingdom through faith in God's love for us.

Power

How a teacher exercises power is an important feature of a teacher's spirituality. Power is a manifestation of the way we influence people. It is a neutral word. Teachers are very powerful people. They can deeply affect the lives of their students for better or worse. When we look back on our schooling, we realise how much power our teachers had. For a Christian teacher, there is the special responsibility of being a mediator of God's gracious love. Power may be considered from the perspective of power over students as responsible stewardship or it may be viewed as control and manipulation. Power may be seen as challenging evil or it may be exercised as an obstruction to healthy change.

For a Christian teacher power is used to influence others to grow and realise the gifts which they possess. Power is liberating, freeing people from their limits of knowledge or low self-esteem. It challenges students to go beyond their present situation and discover new possibilities in wisdom.

The ancient zen warning to teachers is relevant for Christian teachers: 'Beware, beware, lest you trace your patterns on my heart and not see me. 'Teaching which is empowering is disciplined because we have to let go our desire to control and fashion others like myself. My sexuality wishes to create students in my image and likeness. There is some mirror of the divine in each of us. But the poverty and self-renunciation of Christian teaching implies that we seek to nurture our students into maturity, not to trap them into a permanent dependent childhood. At the tomb of Lazarus, Jesus cried out: 'Unbind him, let him go free' (Jn 11:44). This cry to Jesus is powerful theme for every teacher who wishes to be a liberating teacher: 'Unbind them, let them go free!'

Sterility
A serious threat to life and creation spirituality is sterility or stagnation. A teacher can easily become tired, discouraged, and lose any perspective on what should take priority. The inner energising power of the Spirit is suffocated by excessive scheduling and a failure to rest and pray. Creation spirituality cannot be assumed. It needs fostering by many life-giving and -receiving situations and people. A teacher should care for herself and let others love and support her. She may also cultivate avenues of life-giving sources, such as hobbies, sport, films, yoga and Tai'chi, walking, watching TV. A particular source of energy for a Christian teacher is devotion to the Holy Spirit.

Spirit
The Spirit is the source and symbol of life energy in the Christian life. Luke's gospel records Jesus as beginning his public mission with the affirmation of the Spirit:
> Filled with the Holy Spirit, Jesus left the Jordan and was led by the Spirit through the wilderness (Lk 4:1).

Paths and Stories

Jesus consoled the first Christian teachers with a promise of the Spirit:

> ... the Advocate, the Holy Spirit,
> whom the Father will send in my name,
> will teach you everything (Jn 14:26).

The Spirit is the companion of Christian teachers, the 'dabhar' or energy flow of God's creativity. The Spirit enables us to experience adoption as children of God:

> ... for what you received was not the spirit of slavery to bring you back into fear; you received the spirit of adoption, enabling us to cry out, 'Abba, Father!'
> (Rm 8:14-15).

It is consoling to know that the Spirit enables us to persevere in the spiritual life. St Paul describes the power of the Spirit as:

> Now instead of the spirit of the world, we have received the Spirit that comes from God, to teach us to understand the gifts that he has given us (1 Co 2:12).

In the dawning of time, the divine wind (*ruah*) moves across the chaos to bring life and order (Gn 1:2). The mighty wind of God parts the Red Sea (Ex 14:21-31) and enables the Israelites to escape from tyranny to freedom. The spirit of Yahweh generates life in dry bones (Ezk 37). The wind of Pentecost transforms frightened disciples into courageous missionaries (Ac 2).

Devotion to the Holy Spirit is a source of strength to teachers and gives inspiration to the art of teaching. A Spirit teacher is a life teacher.

The teacher as a creation person

REFLECTION

1. Recall some occasions when you felt a sense of life, vitality and creation. What happened?

2. Who has been a 'life-giver' in your teaching career?

   Why have these people been so significant?

3. At the present time, which situations are oppressive or are not life-giving?

4. In your teaching, whom are you now helping to new life?

5. What do you do to enhance yourself as a life-giver?

6. Describe the sabbath times which are helpful to you.

7. What is your understanding of 'creation spirituality'?

Paths and Stories

SCRIPTURE

Luke 7:11-17
Now soon afterwards Jesus went to a town called Nain, accompanied by his disciples and a great number of people. When he was near the gate of the town it happened that a dead man was being carried out for burial, the only son of his mother, and she was a widow. And a considerable number of the townspeople were with her. When the Lord saw her he felt sorry for her. 'Do not cry' he said. Then he went up and put his hand on the bier and the bearers stood still. And he said, 'Young man, I tell you to get up.' And the dead man sat up and began to talk, and Jesus gave him to his mother. Everyone was filled with awe and praised God saying, 'A great prophet has appeared among us; God has visited his people.' And this opinion of him spread throughout Judaea and all over the countryside.

Matthew 28:6
The angel said to the women, 'There is no need for you to be afraid. I know you are looking for Jesus, who was crucified. He is not here, for he has risen, as he said he would.'

Luke 8:49-56
While Jesus was still speaking, someone arrived from the house of the synagogue official to say, 'Your daughter has died. Do not trouble the Master any further.' But Jesus had heard this, and he spoke to the man, 'Do not be afraid, only have faith and she will be safe'. When he came to the house he allowed no one to go in with him except Peter and John and James, and the child's father and mother. They were all weeping and mourning for her, but Jesus said, 'Stop crying; she is not dead, but asleep'. But they laughed at him, knowing she was dead.

But taking her by the hand he called to her, 'Child, get up'. And her spirit returned and she got up at once. Then he told them to give her something to eat. Her parents were astonished, but he ordered them not to tell anyone what had happened.

John 17:7-8
   Jesus said, 'Now at last they know
   that all you have given me comes indeed from you;
   for I have given them
   the teaching you gave to me,
   and they have truly accepted this, that I came from you,
   and have believed that it was you who sent me.'

6

TEACHERS AND THE CROSS

There is a poignant story about a majestic bamboo in a king's palace garden who is asked by the king every day for three days if she will agree to be cut down, to be stripped and then cut in half. On each of the three days, the bamboo weeps in her suffering, yet says 'yes' to the king because she loves the king. The king uses the two halves of the bamboo to take water from the palace lake to an arid field. Soon the arid field blooms with life. The bamboo realises that through her suffering, the arid field became fertile.

The Christian story is like this parable. Jesus never explained the meaning of suffering, he lived it. Mark's gospel portrays Jesus as the Suffering Servant of Isaiah. Jesus, like the Suffering Servant, is mysteriously chosen to suffer for the sake of others. Isaiah describes the redemptive mission of the Servant:

> And yet ours were the sufferings he bore,
> ours the sorrows he carried.
> But we, we thought of him as someone punished,
> struck by God, and brought low.
> Yet he was pierced through for our faults,
> crushed for our sins.
> On him lies a punishment that brings us peace,
> and through his wounds we are healed (Is 53:4-5).

The spirituality of a teacher embraces suffering. There are many faces of suffering in a teacher's life. Apart from her own personal ones, there may be the anguish of seeing the scars of broken children, the false values propagated in society. Sometimes there is a frustration in the lack of student response. There may be a fracturing of relationships among school staff, between administration, parents and children.

What is the response of a Christian teacher to suffering? How does a teacher develop a spirituality of the cross? How does a teacher help his students to transform suffering?

Facing suffering

One of the most important themes in a spirituality of suffering is to confront the pain itself. We must not deny our pain or project it on to someone else. In Luke's gospel it is recorded that Jesus 'resolutely took the road to Jerusalem' (Lk 9:52).

He guessed that the horrors of execution were waiting for him there, but he went bravely forward. It takes courage to look suffering in the face because it tells us about our own mortality and limits. We usually flee from it or distract ourselves. To acknowledge that I have failed or that I am sick or unable to cope is a humbling experience. I like to feel that I am in control of the situation. In suffering, we are not in command. We are challenged to draw from our inner resources to cope. In faith, we also struggle to believe in a loving God even though God's face is hidden. By naming our reality, we become vulnerable to God's grace.

There are many 'little' deaths in our life journey. There is the death of youth, of our ego, of some of our dreams, of some relationships, perhaps of our good health. The cycle of life and death is essential to our humanity. The 'dark night of the soul' is eloquently written about in the spiritual classics, especially in the writings of John of the Cross.

The cross is a symbol of life, not death. The early Christians did not use the cross as a symbol because the brutal reality of crucifixions was too obvious to be a symbol. A spirituality of the cross searches for ways to allow suffering to be transformed into a new depth of our being as children of God. Failure is not intended to be an end but a new beginning, a doorway opening to other rooms of our house. God does not wish suffering. When Christ died, God wept. The God of love is present in our suffering, if we let him remain there. God is compassionate. Being compassionate is to weep with another in solidarity. God's presence in love does not necessarily take away suffering, but gives power to transform it.

We will be hurt by others and others will wound us. Each of us carries the brokenness of being a sinful person, always in need of redemption. The incompleteness within us and our world is the opportunity for dynamic action and growth. Unfortunately, it may also be the occasion for destruction and sterile pain. We make choices all along the way of life. Some of our choices involve suffering.

As a teacher, I have memories of my failures as a teacher. Sometimes, I aroused resentment and anger, not love and learning. I wish I could undo the damage of these times but I cannot. I have a particular memory of an unjust punishment I administered to a student in 1963. Perhaps some day I will meet Peter again and be able to ask his forgiveness. Our anger or the anger of others may be a source of suffering. Anger can be a friend to the spiritual life by channelling creative energy towards change or justice. It is oppressive if it is a weapon to punish or hurt.

Jesus and suffering
Jesus identified with our pain and suffering to offer us a way of transformation. Jesus said:

> Unless a wheat grain falls on the ground and dies,
> it remains only a single grain;
> but if it dies,
> it yields a rich harvest (Jn 12:24).

Jesus feared his 'hour', the experience of his passion. In the trauma of Gethsemane, he begged his Father for escape from its pain: 'Take this cup away from me' (Mk 14:36). All teachers have some 'cups' which they would wish were not to be theirs. A source of suffering may be a breakdown in the relationship with the class, or staff tensions. As a teacher, I may be anxious about my ability to cope or the responsibilities which I have been given. St Paul has encouraging words faltering teachers:

> We are only the earthenware jars that hold this treasure, to make it clear that such an overwhelming power comes from God and not from us. We are in difficulties on all sides, but never cornered; we see no answer to our problems, but never despair; ... always, wherever we may be, we carry with us in our body the death of Jesus, so that the life of Jesus, too, may always be seen in our body' (2 Co 4:7-8,10).

Paradox

In art, Jesus has been portrayed as a clown. That image is perceptive because Jesus does indeed represent the supreme paradox of coming to give life and yet this life was gained for us through a terrifying death. The spirituality of a teacher is involved with the paradox of reconciling the many opposites which are part of the inter-relationships of teaching. The jester symbol is an appropriate one for teachers. There are really no idyllic situations. The jester symbol points to the paradox inherent in being human. As a facilitator of many teaching staffs, I have shared some of the pain of conflict and confrontation which have often helped a group to a new point of understanding as a group. If conflict between a teacher and a student is approached with the Christ inspiration of the possibility of transforming love, then there is some hope of both people seeing new dimensions in the relationships.

Redemptive teaching

Teaching is a redemptive activity. It is inviting people to go beyond the limits of knowledge, personalities and social situations. There is a risk involved in redemptive teaching, both for the teacher and the student. They have to let go of past hurts and the security of fortified positions of always being right.

Suffering erodes our illusion of independence. We become vulnerable in suffering. In redemptive suffering, we let go our ego and allow the 'image of God' centre force to be the axis of our consciousness. God becomes the unifying power in our lives in redemptive suffering, Christ's suffering becomes a model for our own passion.

A Christian approach to suffering is characterised by love and compassion. Students feel a sense of self-worth. They are given space in which to make mistakes. The response to student failure should be to challenge them, not punish them.

Suffering has a communal dimension. The sufferings of our students remind us of our own brokenness. Low self-esteem, anger, anxiety, fear and hatred exhibit many faces. Teachers are aware of their own limits and stand with their students, not in patronising pity, but in solidarity.

The story of the mustard seed is illustrative of the communal nature of suffering.

Once upon a time, a widow's only son died. She went to a holy man and begged him to restore her son's life. He was moved by her anguish and said: 'Bring me a mustard seed from a house which has no suffering and I will restore his life'. So she travelled throughout the great kingdom, visiting house after house in search of the mustard seed. In every house, people shared their stories of suffering. They told of death, illness, debt, divorce and loneliness.

Finally she returned to the holy man and said: 'I have not found a mustard seed but I have been restored to life through recognising that my suffering is shared in different ways by every person. I am not alone in my grief.'

Reconciliation

Redemptive teaching is reconciling the fractured aspects of our relationships with God and the community. Christians know that we should be humbly conscious of God's mercy and saving graciousness. Sin is ever-present within us and our world. Our pleas to God for mercy and reconciliation speak our desire to harmonise the conflicting elements within us. There is suffering in apologising to our students and asking for reconciliation as we invite them into their own positions of forgiveness. Little wonder that Jesus spent so much time with his disciples on the significance of reconciliation. It can be so hard to let go of our anger and hatred towards those who have betrayed us, mocked us, smeared our character. Yet we cannot lay claim to be authentic Christian teachers unless we seek reconciliation. Restoring relationships is redemptive teaching.

The cross is a potent symbol for a Christian teacher. God did not take away the cross of Jesus but raised him up on the third day. Jesus accepted his destiny in trust: 'Father, into your hands I commit my spirit' (Lk 23:46). Suffering does not have a gloomy finality. For a Christian teacher, it is the other face of the resurrection. Failure is the first step to transformation and hope.

REFLECTION

1. Consider some of the paradox situations you are now experiencing.

2. As a teacher, what have been some times of suffering in your life? Comment on other teachers' experiences of suffering.

3. How do you, as a teacher, cope with suffering?
4. What is your reflection on a spirituality of the cross for teachers?

5. What do you do to transform suffering into occasions of growth in your spiritual life?

SCRIPTURE

Luke 9:23
   Then to all Jesus said, 'If anyone wants to be a follower of mine, let him renounce himself and take up his cross every day and follow me.'

Luke 24:25-26
   Then Jesus said to them, 'Was it not ordained that the Christ should suffer and so enter into his glory?'

2 Corinthians 1:8-11
   For we should like you to realise, brothers, that the things we had to undergo in Asia were more of a burden than we could carry, so that we despaired of coming through alive. Yes, we were carrying our own death warrant with us, and it has taught us not to rely on ourselves but only on God, who raises the dead to life. And he saved us from dying, as he will save us again; yes, that is our firm hope in him, that in the future he will save us again. You must all join in the prayers for us; the more people that are asking for help for us, the more will be giving thanks when it is granted to us.

John 20:27
   Jesus came in and stood among them: 'Peace be with you' he said. Then he spoke to Thomas, 'Put your finger here; look, here are my hands. Give me your hand; put it into my side. Doubt no longer but believe.'

7

THE TEACHER AS A CARING PERSON

A teacher's vocation is one of action. A prime focus for a teacher's spirituality is service to his students. The teacher prepares lessons, supervises sporting fixtures, teaches in a classroom and corrects papers. This service should express enthusiasm for promoting God's love for every person.

The image of shepherd is a popular symbol for teacher in the Bible. A teacher's care for her students is known as 'pastoral care'. If a teacher's spirituality is relational with students and other people in the educational community, then pastoral care expresses the fruits of the Lord's presence working through the gifts of the teacher to serve her students.

By pastoral care we mean care for people in the spirit of the shepherd model of Jesus. 'I am the good shepherd' (Jn 10:14). The shepherd is faithful. He is courageous in the face of adversity. He knows the sheep by name and is prepared to go to extreme lengths when a sheep has wandered to dangerous places (Lk 15:4-7).

Through pastoral care, the teacher enters the mystery of the Trinity, a mystery of communion. When we think about the Trinity, we appreciate that the very nature of God is relational in community and there is an equality of persons. Women and men are created in the image of a God who is social and dynamic. This dynamic communion is centred on the divine creative energy of love. 'God is love' (1 Jn 4:16). Paul eloquently describes how love is the climax of all Christian activity:

Love is always patient and kind; it is never jealous; love is never boastful or conceited; it is never rude or selfish; it does not take offence, and is not resentful. Love takes no pleasure in other people's sins but delights in the truth; it is always ready to excuse, to trust, to hope and to endure whatever comes. Love does not come to an end (1 Co 13:4-8).

Love is an expression of oneself which brings life to another. A Christian teacher is one who loves her students. She may not feel love but her actions will demonstrate the quality of love.

Love involves an extension of self. It is not denying self because Christian love means loving oneself as well as another. We are able to love joyfully when we are conscious of God's unconditional love for us. Our love overflows to our sisters and brothers as an extension of our being loved. This 'kenosis' follows the self-giving of Jesus.

> His state was divine
> yet he did not cling
> to his equality with God
> but emptied himself
> to assume the condition of a slave (Ph 2:6-7).

Every teacher knows how much it costs to love his students. A genuine love for students is a disciplined relationship. Renunciation in love need not be inhibiting but should set boundaries for an energy flow between people. We don't have to use our energy to preserve our ego status. We give love to receive it. Jesus said: 'Anyone who loses his life for my sake, will save it' (Lk 9:24).

The Beatitudes
The eight Beatitudes (Mt 5:3-12) reflect the paradox of Christian relationships. Service with love leads to the

inheritance of the Kingdom. The Beatitudes are a charter for the quality of pastoral care of a Christian teacher. Each of them describes a dimension of true relationships:

Happy are the poor in spirit: theirs is the Kingdom of heaven.	Happy are they who acknowledge their dependence on God and other people.
Happy the gentle: they shall have the earth for their heritage.	Happy are they who do not manipulate others and give space to others.
Happy those who mourn: they shall be comforted.	Happy are those who share another's sorrow.
Happy those who hunger and thirst for what is right: they shall be satisfied.	Happy are those who work for justice.
Happy the merciful: they shall have mercy shown them.	Happy are those who show compassion.
Happy the pure in heart: they shall see God.	Happy are those who establish right priorities in their lives.
Happy the peacemakers: they shall be called sons of God.	Happy are those who work for reconciliation.
Happy those who are persecuted in the cause of right: theirs is the kingdom of heaven.	Happy are those who are willing to pay a price for justice.

The Beatitudes are the new covenant of relationships. They were collected from the various teachings of Jesus and shared by Matthew's early community as a summary of the spirit of discipleship. The values inherent in the Beatitudes stand in contradiction to world values of control and manipulation in relationships. A teacher might select one Beatitude for each week and explore the meaning of the Beatitude for his spiritual life. For example, he may examine the Beatitude of being a peacemaker and apply it to the policies of the school or the interactions between students and teachers.

Compassion
Compassion is a consequence of love. Compassion is weeping with the other. The Hebrew word is related to womb, bringing forth life and mercy. It implies a solidarity whereby the teacher reaches out to his students to say: 'I, too, need love, challenge, affirmation and healing'. He is companion and partner in the vicissitudes of life. Compassion does not accept a superior-inferior relationship. Christian compassion acknowledges that we all need the saving graciousness of God. The prayer of the 'Our Father' binds our common humanity into the triangle of reconciliation. Our reconciliation with others is linked with our reconciliation with God. Compassion recognises that our destiny is mutual, not individual. An ancient Hindu saying describes this mutuality of compassion:

> I looked into the distance
> and saw something moving.
> I thought it was an animal.
> When it came closer,
> I saw it was a man.
> When I looked into his eyes,
> I saw it was my brother.

The last judgement scene as portrayed by Matthew (Mt 25:31-46) reminds us that we see the face of God in the faces of the outsiders and dispossessed of society. When we are compassionate, we share in the mercy of God.

Compassion is risky business. We are not sure if others want our care or are secure enough with us to respond. They may view it as patronage or establishing dependency. To extend the hand of compassion is to be vulnerable. Some students may interpret a teacher's compassion as a sign of weakness and scorn it.

Reciprocal pastoral care
Pastoral care is reciprocal. We don't give service on any assumption that the other person has no human resources. That would be a kind of banking style of pastoral care which would imply: 'This poor person has nothing and is so needy. So I'll be kind and from my bounty will look after him'. When a teacher is acting in a helping role, she should be asking herself: 'What is the gift which this student is giving me now?' The poor can evangelise us if we listen and accept their gift to us. Every pastoral carer is a wounded healer. Our own revealed limits encourage others to share their failures because they know we also have visited places of sorrow.

Harmony
Pastoral care is action for justice. Wherever there is dislocation of harmony in human relationships, resources of food, clothing, housing, then the Body of Christ is affronted. Action for justice is not a panacea for violence, sickness, unemployment or disabilities. Suffering remains a mystery of our mortality. The First Song of the Servant of Yahweh is an inspiring passage for a teacher's commitment to justice:

Here is my servant whom I uphold,
my chosen one in whom my soul delights.
I have endowed him with my spirit
that he may bring true justice to the nations.

Faithfully he brings true justice;
he will neither waver, nor be crushed
until true justice is established on earth,
for the islands are awaiting his law. (Is 42:1, 4)

A teacher's spirituality should embrace some of the dream for a restoration of harmony in the world 'until true justice is established on earth'.

Presence
The gift of presence is a simple but profound dimension of a spirituality of pastoral care. We are present to another by listening, by observing, by sharing or by our silence. Sometimes we don't need words to be present, just being together is enough to express companionship. It's like that with God. At times we pray, say psalms, sing, dance, participate in the sacraments, at other times we just sit and be still, allowing the Presence to fill our being. Teachers are present to students in so many ways, for example, by chit-chat in the school yard, bus supervision, in class or on the sporting field. Pastoral presence is attentive presence. Such presence does not intend to capture another emotionally or intellectually, it is content to be about, to waste time, to allow the other to feel respected in resting from having to speak or work. In our culture, the gift of being present might be regarded with some suspicion because it does not seem to be productive or profitable. Perhaps the highest compliment a student might pay to a teacher would be that she 'used to be about with us when we were doing nothing'.

Community

The development of the Christian community is the context and environment for pastoral care. A Christian teacher's spirituality is communal in its setting. The feeling of belonging and being 'home' are important constituents of community. People in the community celebrate, not just the joyful occasions, but the sad ones as well. One of my most moving experiences was with a 'Faith and Light' group celebration in Manila's central prison. The singing and obvious joy were combined with the paradox of the sadness of the prison backdrop and the helplessness of some of the more severely disabled people.

The Christian community through its stories, customs and rituals of celebrations, wishes to sanctify the various life moments of its members. The climate of care in the school community should be almost tangible in the way people greet each other and learn together. Through co-operation, the school community can avoid the anxiety of having to compete to establish one's identity. An environment which is affirming and personal is healing. The community in its turn shapes the form of the teacher's spirituality.

Prayer

For a Christian teacher pastoral care is linked with prayer and liturgy. In the letter to the Philippians, we read:

> I thank my God whenever I think of you; and every time I pray for all of you, I pray with joy' (Ph 1:3-4).

In the letter to the Thessalonians, Paul's prayer is: 'May the Lord be generous in increasing your love and make you love one another and the whole human race as much as we love you' (1 Th 3:12). Teachers should pray for their students. The practice of keeping a list of students in a Mass or service book is a useful one to remind the teacher to pray regularly for her students. Whenever possible, the teacher and students should have liturgy and prayer services together. Growing in love and compassion is a faith experience. A Christian community is bonded by faith and the religious bond is deepened by prayer. We pray for unity (Jn 17:21), for our daily bread and for forgiveness (Mt 6:10-13).

Christ as a model for pastoral care

Our appreciation of pastoral care has been greatly assisted by the insights of psychology and therapy. While we recognise the contributions of the social sciences to our pastoral care practices, the Christian teacher knows that Christ is the ultimate reference for our humanity. The enterprise of pastoral care in a school or Church agency aspires to be faithful to the Christian vision of men and women created in the image of God. Jesus represents the possibilities and hopes for humankind. After the fifth century, there was more emphasis on Christ as Redeemer, saving us from sin. The sin-redemption theme tended to influence spirituality and its heritage was a negative view of women and men as being born in original sin. Jesus is indeed a Redeemer. However he is first a reminder of our humanity. He reminds us who we are and who we might become. Christian pastoral care situates its philosophy explicitly on the person of Jesus. Through our imagination we create new visions for our destiny and those of our students.

Faithful pastoral care

Most pastoral care activity involves doing routine tasks well. Pastoral care is incarnational when it arises from the belief that the Lord's grace is offered during the course of each day. Most pastoral care is very unspectacular. The hidden life at Nazareth suggest that much of the saving mission of Jesus was accomplished through quiet labour.

Paths and Stories

Pastoral care is faithful to the students. Fidelity is characteristic of authentic care. We are punctual, we are loyal, we try to be patient and we don't panic and opt out when trouble comes. The good shepherd does not take flight at the first sign of conflict (Jn 10:11-13). Sometimes students seem interested and involved, at other times they are disruptive and alienated. God's fidelity to us is a source of comfort and a challenge to our consistency. Isaiah expresses the divine faithfulness:

> Does a woman forget her baby at the breast,
> Or fail to cherish the son of her womb?
> Yet even if these forget,
> I will never forget you.
>
> See, I have branded you on the palms of my hands.
> (Is 49:15-16)

Teaching is leading students to become artists for a renewed society. Pastoral care affirms the gifts of our students to want to be part of the new story of the earth. A teacher's spirituality may be evaluated by the ways in which her encounters with the Lord are translated into action for pastoral care. Jesus said:

> You will be able to tell them by their fruits. (Mt 7:16)

REFLECTION

1. What do you understand by the term 'pastoral care?'

2. In what ways have you exercised pastoral care?

3. How is pastoral care related to the spirituality of a teacher?

4. In what ways are faith and prayer integral to pastoral care for the teacher?

5. How does a teacher love her students?

6. Who cares for you?

Paths and Stories

SCRIPTURE

Isaiah 43:2-3
    Do not be afraid, for I have redeemed you;
    I have called you by your name, you are mine.
    Should you pass through the sea, I will be with you;
    or through rivers, they will not swallow you up.
    Should you walk through fire, you will not be scorched
    and the flames will not burn you.
    For I am Yahweh, your God,
    the Holy One of Israel, your saviour.

John 10:11, 14-15
    Jesus said, 'I am the good shepherd:
    the good shepherd is one who lays down his life for his sheep.
    I am the good shepherd; I know my own
    and my own know me,
    just as the Father knows me
    and I know the Father;
    and I lay down my life for my sheep.'

Luke 19:1-10
    Jesus entered Jericho and was going through the town when a man whose name was Zacchaeus made his appearance; he was one of the senior tax collectors and a wealthy man. He was anxious to see what kind of man Jesus was, but he was too short and could not see him for the crowd; so he ran ahead and climbed a sycamore tree to catch a glimpse of Jesus who was to pass that way. When Jesus reached the spot he looked up and spoke to him: 'Zacchaeus, come down. Hurry, because I must stay at your house today.' And he hurried down and welcomed him joyfully. They all complained when they saw what was happening. 'He has gone to stay at a sinner's house', they said. But Zacchaeus stood his

The teacher as a caring person

ground and said to the Lord, 'Look, sir, I am going to give half my property to the poor, and if I have cheated anybody I will pay him back four times the amount.' And Jesus said to him, 'Today salvation has come to this house, because this man too is a son of Abraham; for the Son of Man has come to seek out and save what was lost.'

Isaiah 54:10
    The mountains may depart
    the hills be shaken,
    but my love for you will never leave you
    and my covenant of peace with you
    will never be shaken
    says Yahweh who takes pity on you.

8

THE TEACHER AS ONE WHO IS CALLED

The focus of this chapter is to consider how a teacher's spirituality may be related to the idea of vocation. In consumer societies, work is useful because it earns money enabling us to buy more goods. Against such prevailing cultural values, it takes some effort for a teacher to see Christian teaching as a vocation to continue the creative energy of the Spirit in the world. There is no suggestion that wages are not important in this enterprise. For professional teachers, appropriate salaries pay bills and reduce mortgages. One of the features of Christian teaching over the centuries has been the belief that it is a vocation. A Christian teacher is one who has been chosen and called. Isaiah has a poetic description of the calling of a teacher:

> Here is my servant whom I uphold,
> My chosen one in whom my soul delights.
> I have endowed him with my spirit
> that he may bring true justice to the nations (Is 42:1).

and again:

> I, Yahweh, have called you to serve the cause of right;
> I have taken you by the hand and formed you;
> I have appointed you as covenant of the people
> and light of the nations,
> to open the eyes of the blind,
> to free captives from prison,
> and those who live in darkness from the dungeon.
>
> (Is 42:6-7)

The teacher as one who is called

For many teachers, this calling may not be so obvious. There are many motives which lead people to teach. They may be invited to teach in Sunday school or in the parish, they may like the idea of working in a Christian school, they may wish to follow in the footsteps of family or peers who have chosen to teach. The sense of vocation may be mixed with the attitude of being an employee in a system of education. Although there is no conflict in theory between being a member of a teacher's union and participating in teaching as vocation, in practice there may be some tensions, particularly if there are fragile relations between the union and the employers.

Jesus invited people to follow him and missioned his disciples to teach. Luke describes one such occasion when a group of fishermen chose to go with Jesus after the startling miracle of netting a huge number of fish (Lk 5:1-11). Jesus said 'Do not be afraid; from now on it is people you will catch' (Lk 5:10).

Mary as one who was chosen and called

The scenario of the annunciation story presents us with a way of exploring the nature of vocation. Mary is portrayed as the first disciple. She is also the first teacher of Jesus. By considering the movements of the story (Lk 1:26-42), we may appreciate the spirituality of vocation.

> In the sixth month the angel Gabriel was sent by God to a town in Galilee called Nazareth (26), to a virgin betrothed to a man named Joseph, of the House of David: and the virgin's name was Mary (27). He went in and said to her, 'Rejoice, so highly favoured! The Lord is with you' (28). She was deeply disturbed by these words and asked herself what this greeting could mean (29), but the angel said to her, 'Mary, do not be afraid; you have won God's favour. Listen! (30) You are to conceive and bear a son, and you must name him Jesus (31). He

Paths and Stories

will be great and will be called Son of the Most High (32). The Lord God will give him the throne of his ancestor David; he will rule over the House of Jacob for ever and his reign will have no end' (33). Mary said to the angel, 'But how can this come about, since I am a virgin?' (34) 'The Holy Spirit will come upon you' the angel answered 'and the power of the Most High will cover you with its shadow (35). And so the child will be holy and will be called Son of God (36). Know this too: your kinswoman Elizabeth has, in her old age, herself conceived a son, and she whom people called barren is now in her sixth month, for nothing is impossible to God' (37). 'I am the handmaid of the Lord', said Mary 'let what you have said be done to me.' And the angel left her (38).

Mary set out at that time and went as quickly as she could to a town in the hill country of Judah (39). She went into Zechariah's house and greeted Elizabeth (40). Now as soon as Elizabeth heard Mary's greeting, the child leapt in her womb (41) and Elizabeth was filled with the Holy Spirit' (42).

Consider the movement of the story as:

Movement	*Teaching as Vocation*
1. *Life situation* Verses 26-27	Teachers belong to particular times in history and in cultures.
2. *Blessing* Verse 28	God wishes to announce a blessing on teachers and their gifts.
3. *Anxiety* Verses 29-31	Teachers might become anxious at the responsibility: 'Can I do it?'

4. *Invitation* Verses 31-34	Teachers are invited to be life-giving people, to be generative.
5. *Paradox* Verse 35	The teacher may ask: 'Do I have what it takes to be a Christian teacher?'
6. *Reassurance* Verses 35-37	God affirms the teacher: 'You can be a life person through the power of the Spirit. Just look what I've done through other people.'
7. *Trustful acceptance* Verse 38	The 'fiat' of the teacher is saying 'yes' to the invitation.
8. *Mission* Verses 39-42	The teacher embarks on a mission to teach and the action of the Spirit is continued in others as it was in Elizabeth.

These eight movements of the annunciation story suggest a way of looking at the spirituality of vocation. Mary could have prayed for a miracle. Instead she opened herself to the creative presence of the Spirit by saying 'Yes'. A teacher is conscious of her limitations but is prepared to engage in teaching, trusting in the life-giving powers of the Holy Spirit.

The 'Magnificat' of Mary is also a model for a spirituality of vocation. In reflecting on this prayer, we identify three themes:

Paths and Stories

1. *Vocation*

God works through those who are open to God's presence.	And Mary said: 'My soul proclaims the greatness of the Lord and my spirit exults in God my saviour; because he has looked upon his lowly handmaid. Yes, from this day forward all generations will call me blessed, for the Almighty has done great things for me. Holy is his name, and his mercy reaches from age to age for those who fear him.'

2. *Justice*

The special focus of a teaching vocation is to promote justice.	He has shown the power of his arm, he has routed the proud of heart. He has pulled down princes from their thrones and exalted the lowly. The hungry he has filled with good things, the rich sent empty away.

3. *Remembering*

God's promise of mercy and care is our reassurance.	He has come to the help of Israel his servant, mindful of his mercy – according to the promise he made to our descendants for ever.

The 'Magnificat' is a prayer about the vocation to justice. In the spirit of this prayer, the teacher might reflect how he has accomplished great things in the past to support students. Through the promise of God's help, he is confident of continuing this work in the future. He may be very gifted as teacher but he knows that Christian education is a co-operative enterprise between God and himself and many others. He wishes to have a special concern for marginalised students and parents. In the Bible, the widow and the orphan are symbols of the oppressed. God's promise to Abraham and his people reminds us that God is a faithful God.

Biblical vocations
The Bible relates the stories of vocation callings to many people. Jeremiah is appointed as prophet. He protests his inadequacy but Yahweh encourages him with a promise to protect him and inspire his message to the nations (Jr 1:4-10).

Perhaps later in his life when he was being hounded and persecuted he must have wondered whether he had dreamt the whole vocation thing. The story of Samuel's vocation is delightful account of God's loving persistence in asking Samuel to be his messenger (1 S 3:1-12). Three times Samuel comes running in to Eli, believing that Eli has summoned him. On the fourth occasion, Samuel realises that it is Yahweh who is calling and responds: 'Speak, Yahweh, your servant is listening' (1 S 3:9).

Teaching as ministry
In early Christianity, teaching was included in the various ministries of service to the Christian community. Over the centuries, the primal tradition of ministry was gradually restricted to ordination. Since Vatican II, there has been a rapid expansion in the scope and exercise of ministries. Teaching was one of the most important ministries in the Church of the New Testament (1 Co 12:8). The ministry of teaching originated in the commission to preach the Good News. Matthew's gospel concludes with the missioning of the disciples:

> Go therefore, make disciples of all the nations; baptise them in the name of the Father and of the Son and of the Holy Spirit, and teach them to observe all the commands I gave you. And know that I am with you always; yes, to the end of time (Mt 28:19-20).

All ministry is related to the evangelising activity of the community and is accountable to it. A teacher involved in Christian education participates in the teaching mission of the Church. He should exercise care to be faithful to the wisdom of the Christian community and not engage in the propagation of his own beliefs when they are clearly in contradiction to the Church. This matter is a delicate one requiring great sensitivity so that the conscience of the individual is safeguarded. However, if the teacher is employed by a Church agency, then he has a responsibility to support the ethos and beliefs of the Christian community.

To engage in the ministry of teaching is to mediate grace. It is to proclaim the values of the reign of God. Teaching as ministry is revealing the wholeness of knowledge. It is a sacramental experience by which the teacher explores wisdom from a perspective of transcendental values. Christian teaching is a vocation to pursue truth, not in a series of propositions but in authentic personal relationships with ourselves, with Christ the source of truth, with the community and with the world. In a certain sense, the ministry of teaching is an attempt to restore right relationships. The prayer of Jesus, 'consecrate them in the truth; that they may be one as we are one' (Jn 17:17,22), is an appropriate prayer for all teachers. Restoration of right relationships in truth will open us to a commitment to honest dealings with our students. It will ask us to be careful and discerning in our speech and to acknowledge that by listening, we gain further access to truth. Authenticity will be a bond between teachers and students.

The teacher as one who is called

Teaching as ministry continues the cycle of the Word (Is 55:10-11) throughout the world. Teaching is sowing the seed of the Word (Mk 4:1-10). In the prevailing industrial climate, it is a struggle to avoid reducing the concept of vocation to merely a job for wages. The mind-set of a 'them versus us' attitude in the educational structures may generate alienation towards employers. Teaching then becomes a job to be done within the context of an employer-employee dichotomy. While membership of an independent teacher's union can be very beneficial to a teacher's welfare, it is imperative that the industrial and vocational models of participating in Christian education are in accord with gospel values of justice and reconciliation. The development of a teacher's spirituality would be impeded if his energies were diverted to confrontations with employing authorities. School employing groups should ensure that there is a positive industrial climate in any school system.

Service is a key element in appreciating teaching as ministry. Jesus gave his life as a gift for our salvation. This value of service contrasts with the materialistic view which insists that everything has its price. Such an attitude says that there is no such thing as something for nothing. Everything is to be weighed out in monetary terms. While there must always be a legitimate expectation of just wages for professional teachers, the Christ example of washing feet in service should be an integral feature of a Christian teacher's spirituality. There are so many occasions for service when we are teaching, such as helping a student who can't cope with studies, comforting a child who is broken by family strife, patiently working through problems with adults on a course. To serve is to share in the sacrifice of Jesus in giving himself for others. In the first letter of Peter we read:

Each one of you has received a special grace, so, like

good stewards responsible for all these different graces of God, put yourselves at the service of others. If you are a speaker, speak in words which seem to come from God; if you are a helper, help as though every action was done at God's orders; so that in everything God may receive the glory, through Jesus Christ, since to him alone belong all glory and power for ever and ever. Amen (1 P 4:10-11).

I believe that a significant aspect of spirituality for a teacher is a deepening awareness of being called by God to teach. The awareness involves an appreciation of the privilege of being a teacher. Teaching as a vocation generates an enthusiasm for the art of teaching. It challenges us as teachers to understand better what Christian teaching means. The power of the Spirit is there to give us insight to our ministry. Paul writes to the Corinthians:

Now instead of the spirit of the world, we have received the Spirit that comes from God, to teach us to understand the gifts that he has given us. Therefore we teach, not in the way in which philosophy is taught, but in the way that the Spirit teaches us: we teach spiritual things spiritually (1 Co 2:12-14).

REFLECTION

1. Have you experienced a sense of calling to be a teacher? If so, when and in what circumstances did you feel called?

2. Have you ever experienced tension between the job of teaching and the vocation of teaching?

3. Which famous teachers throughout history seemed to have a strong sense of calling or vocation?

4. What do you understand by the term 'ministry of teaching?'

5. How might the work of teaching be seen as a spiritual activity?

SCRIPTURE

Isaiah 6:1-8

In the year of King Uzziah's death I saw the Lord Yahweh seated on a high throne; his train filled the sanctuary; above him stood seraphs, each one with six wings: two to cover its face, two to cover its feet and two for flying.

> And they cried out one to another in this way,
> 'Holy, holy, holy is Yahweh Sabaoth.
> His glory fills the whole earth.'

The foundations of the threshold shook with the voice of the one who cried out, and the Temple was filled with smoke. I said:

> 'What a wretched state I am in! I am lost,
> for I am a man of unclean lips
> and I live among a people of unclean lips,
> and my eyes have looked at the King, Yahweh Sabaoth.'

Then one of the seraphs flew to me, holding in his hand a live coal which he had taken from the altar with a pair of tongs. With this he touched my mouth, and said:
> 'See now, this has touched your lips,
> your sin is taken away,
> your iniquity is purged.'

Then I heard the voice of the Lord saying:

> 'Whom shall I send? Who will be our messenger?'
> I answered,
> 'Here I am, send me'.

The teacher as one who is called

1 *Corinthians 3:5-14*

After all, what is Apollos and what is Paul? They are servants who brought the faith to you. Even the different ways in which they brought it were assigned to them by the Lord. I did the planting, Apollos did the watering, but God made things grow. Neither the planter nor the waterer matters: only God, who makes things grow. It is all one who does the planting and who does the watering, and each will duly be paid according to his share in the work. We are fellow workers with God; you are God's farm, God's building.

By the grace God gave me, I succeeded as an architect and laid the foundations, on which someone else is doing the building. Everyone doing the building must work carefully. For the foundation, nobody can lay any other than the one which has already been laid, that is Jesus Christ. On this foundation you can build in gold, silver and jewels, or in wood, grass and straw, but whatever the material, the work of each builder is going to be clearly revealed when the day comes. That day will begin with fire, and the fire will test the quality of each man's work. If his structure stands up to it, he will get his wages; if it is burnt down, he will be the loser, and though he is saved himself, it will be as one who has gone through fire.

9

CONTINUING THE JOURNEY

We all know the fable about the race between the hare and the tortoise. The fleet hare was so confident he was far ahead in the race against the tortoise that he went to sleep on the roadside and lost the race. The story of our spirituality is like this race. It is a dynamic process. We never say that we have made it, we have arrived, but rather that we are on the way.

The spirituality of a Christian teacher is the core of meaning from which teaching activities flow. It is a unifying focus for the teacher's ministry. Her role is to pursue the search for knowledge and wisdom from the perspective of God's love for us in Jesus.

The following suggestions in this chapter are proposed as aids to enhance the spirituality of teachers.

Contemplation
A Zen story is told about the need for contemplation. Once a monk was riding a galloping horse. As the horse and rider thundered past, an old farmer sitting on a gate called out: 'Sir, where are you going?' The monk yelled out as he flashed by: 'Don't ask me, ask the horse!'

Through contemplation we develop the space to remember God's mercy to us and to rearrange our priorities. The pressures of our work and social life may cause us to live only in the present. Our perception of time is significant in our way of relating to others and our world.

We live in three kinds of time. 'Chronos' is measured time. 'Kairos' is sacred moment time and 'mystical' or 'dreaming time' is time to dwell religiously with our myths and stories. Since the advent of clocks after the sixteenth century, the technological world is so locked into 'chronos' time that it has almost lost the awareness of 'kairos' and 'mystical' time. To engage in contemplation teachers should develop an appreciation of 'kairos' time, learning to pause to savour precious moments of a smile, a sunset, a marvel of technology. The whole of the earth is a sacrament of God's presence. Much of God's revelation to us is as a series of whispers from the most unexpected places. If we are faith people who are ready to celebrate the presence of God, then we will certainly discover those moments of grace.

In prayer we express our relationship with the Lord. Prayer should lead us to the still point of our being. In prayer we seek to surrender our being to allow God's love to transform our lives.

For most Christian teachers, there are opportunities to pray with the students on such occasions as chapel services, Mass, morning prayer, assembly prayer and prayer sessions. The cultivation of prayer styles in home and school life is more complex than a participation in class or school prayer sessions. However, if we have a commitment to prayer, then we will always find some avenues for prayer. Often we may not feel like praying but if prayer is a high priority in our lives, then we will certainly pray. For example, we may learn to make a morning offering while having a shower, a prayer of blessing before a meal, to pause in prayer before a difficult interview with a student, to play a taped psalm reading while driving home from work. According to different personalities, prayer styles will be varied. Some may prefer formal prayers like the 'Our Father', others may use mantra prayer forms, or singing, or the Psalms. But whatever the prayer style we use, we strive to involve our whole selves in the enterprise of praying. Prayer has been described as 'standing before God with the mind in the heart'.

Paths and Stories

The Eucharist is the summit of Christian prayer. The Eucharist draws together the past, present and future of the new covenant in Jesus. Through the Eucharist, we enter the mystery of God with us. The communion of the Eucharist is communion with the people of the world and the earth. Whenever possible, a Christian teacher should participate in some kind of eucharistic service and, more particularly, on Sunday. The bread of the Eucharist is linking us to earth and the hungers of the world. The wine of the Eucharist is the cup of our thirst for God and God's dwelling among the people.

Suggestions for praying

1. Resolve to pray regularly.
2. Select a rhythm of prayer some time during the day or week when you might have the opportunity to pray.
3. Become accustomed to praying during ordinary daily tasks.
4. Relax for some time each day, allow the tensions to slip away from you. Try to discover your 'quiet space' places.
5. Let your imagination take you to encounter situations with Jesus. Dialogue with him about your life.
6. Read the Bible regularly. Savour your favourite passages and explore them for new insights.
7. Gather some favourite prayer sayings such as: 'My Lord and my God', 'Come Lord Jesus, come', 'Courage, it is I'. Say them often.
8. Try to orient the ordinary events of your day to the Lord.
9. Say some formal prayers often, e.g. the Rosary, the Psalms, the Office.
10. Participate in liturgical celebrations, e.g. the Mass, divine service.

Continuing the journey

11. Reflect on your life, especially at passage times such as the new year, birth of a child, death of a friend, birthday celebrations.
12. Celebrate with joy the various gifts possessed by you and others.

Commitment to the way
The spiritual life is a serious quest. It is so central to one's vocation that it cannot be left to chance. Two parables of Jesus speak out the priority of finding the Kingdom:

> The Kingdom of heaven is like treasure hidden in a field which someone has found; he hides it again, goes off happy, sells everything he owns and buys the field
> (Mt 13:44).

> The Kingdom of heaven is like a merchant looking for fine pearls; when he finds one of great value he goes and sells everything he owns and buys it (Mt 13:44-45).

Early Christians called the journey of discipleship the 'Way'. One learns to be patient in pursuing the Way. The yeast and seed are apt symbols. The Kingdom of God takes its own time. We can get very impatient for things to happen. Later we realise that we were not ready to move at that stage in our life. If we listen to the seasons of our life, then grace is given according to our levels of readiness. We must not lose courage. There is a vivid description of the spiritual journey in Deuteronomy:

> 'And I said to you: Do not take fright, do not be afraid of them. Yahweh your God goes in front of you and will be fighting on your side as you saw him fight for you in Egypt. In the wilderness, too, you saw him: how Yahweh carried you, as a man carries his child, all along the road you travelled on the way to this place. But for all this,

you put no faith in Yahweh your God, who had gone in front of you on the journey to find you a camping ground, by night in the fire to light your path, by day in the cloud' (Dt 1:29-33).

The images of 'wilderness', 'man carries his child', 'travelled', 'camping ground', 'fire to light your path', 'day in the cloud', are evocative symbols to describe features of the spiritual journey.

Today there are many resources available to assist one on the spiritual journey. According to family circumstances and the teaching situation, a teacher should participate in some religious exercises each year. Examples of available religious exercises might be: spiritual reading, community services to the poor, making a retreat, spiritual direction, listening to religious tapes, joining a prayer group in the parish, having a review of life each month.

Sacramentality

Sacramentality is discovering God in the ordinary events of our day. Sacramentality is approaching people and the world with a sense of the sacred. We try to acknowledge the presence of God wherever we are. The command of Yahweh to Moses: 'Take off your shoes, for the place on which you stand is holy ground' (Ex 3:6), is an injunction which we might all heed. The place on which we stand, with our families, in the classroom, with a Sunday school class, all these and many other places of our teaching and life are holy places for the person of faith. We can learn to be aware of God's presence while enjoying a meal, preparing a class, driving a car, walking, on a picnic, grieving at an act of violence. Our conscious attention is absorbed by the task at hand, but the numinous mystery of the Lord is with us. We know, without being able to specify how and where, God is present.

There are not two realms of existence, the world of the

Spirit and the secular world. This notion is dualistic and gnostic. Religious believers are overwhelmed by the mystery of God's pervading presence. Psalm 139 describes in poetic imagery, the loving attention of God for us:

> Where could I go to escape your spirit?
> Where could I flee from your presence?
> If I climb to the heavens, you are there,
> There too, if I lie in Sheol.
>
> If I flew to the point of sunrise,
> or westward across the sea,
> your hand would still be guiding me,
> your right hand holding me.
>
> It was you who created my inmost self,
> and put me together in my mother's womb;
> for all these mysteries I thank you;
> for the wonder of myself, for the wonder of your works (7-10; 13-14).

Nature time
Our understanding about ourselves is closely related to the way we respond to our natural environment. We are earth people. If we are excited about earth, then we are aware of the possibilities of new discoveries within us. Elizabeth Browning writes about this sense of awe with nature:

> All the earth is holy ground
> and every common bush afire with God.
> Only those who see take off their shoes;
> the rest sit around and pluck berries.

For spirituality, we need to have a love affair with nature, allowing the glory of creation to penetrate our whole being. One day we might stand on a hill and feel the wind blowing us, snatching at our hats, bending reeds and scattering leaves. We can let our eyes travel across the night sky and feel drawn into the canopy of stars; we might become hypnotised by the creaming surf rippling across the mirror sands. In such nature kairos moments, we let go our scientific analysis of wind, sky and sea and are seduced by the music and dance of creation. G.K. Chesterton wrote: 'The world will never starve for wonders, but only for the want of wonder'. Perhaps only when we participate in nature will we recognise that the final reality is mystery. If a teacher's spirituality includes presence with and in nature, then she may be transformed by this experience. God's covenant was made with us and the world (Gn 9). When we invite the sea, a tree, the sky, a mountain to enter our presence, or when we enter theirs, then we are more fully involved in God's holy covenant.

The spirituality of unifaction is sensitive to the oneness and interrelatedness of all things. By this holistic spirituality, we become part of the energy of the cosmic creation of God.

Facing stress
We live in an anxious era. Stress-related diseases take a heavy toll. We are bombarded with noise, consumer pressures drive us to work longer, family relationships are fractured, we crave personal fulfilment – whatever that means. Some teachers experience 'burnout', a feeling of great inner tiredness and loss of meaning. Psychologists such as Freud, Jung, Sullivan, Rank and Horney have discussed the phenomenon of anxiety. Depression and anxiety are deadly enemies of the spiritual life unless they are faced and transformed. The Bible has stories of people who were called to let go of their securities and trust in God. That is always a big risk because we don't know what's at the bottom of the free fall.

Jeremiah, Abraham, Peter, Moses and Paul were moved

to say a big 'yes' to God with trust. After the entry of Jesus into Jerusalem on Palm Sunday, he faced his coming passion in trust:

> Now my soul is troubled.
> What shall I say:
> Father, save me from this hour?
> But it was for this very reason that I have come
> to this hour (Jn 12:27).

If a teacher observes evidence of excessive anxiety and 'burnout' symptoms, she should take immediate steps to rest and develop strategies for reducing tension. Hopefully our identities as teachers are not linked with the myth of busyness which says we have to be in a perpetual whirl to be worthwhile.

Some of our inner tensions arise from the conflict between the 'outer' and 'inner' persons. Jung calls the 'outer' person the 'persona', the role identity which we assume. As parent, teacher, administrator, friend, member, we have many roles in life, but an over-emphasis on our role and neglect of our inner self may lead to the tyranny of the person. By tyranny I mean that the fulfilment of our roles controls our life to such an extent that we neglect the nurturing of our inner life. Jung speaks about establishing the right relationships between 'No.1 man (or woman)' and 'No.2 man (or woman)'. The parable of the two sons (Lk 15:11-32) may be regarded as a story about the relationships between the two faces, the person (elder son) of law and obligation and the inner face of our broken selves (youngest son).

Connecting the outer life and the 'Imago Dei' at the core of our being is a life process towards harmony and *shalom*. We have the feeling of coming home. Spirituality seeks to establish this harmony. Sin is an impediment towards the right relationships of centreing our being on God. 'Attend with listening heart' is a very ancient dictum for spirituality. By attending to our fears and anxieties, we may face them courageously through the power of the Spirit.

Together in community
Christian discipleship is experienced in community. Jesus gathered a community to announce the Good News. The quality of *koinonia* or community was to be a witness to the gospel values of love and reconciliation. A teacher needs to seek out some viable Christian community group which supports and affirms her Christian discipleship. The community may be parish, prayer group, staff of a school or family cluster group. Secular values are so openly espoused in our society that our Christian vision is easily eroded by materialism. The Christian community is a presence of Jesus to its members: 'Where two or three meet in my name, I shall be there with them' (Mt 18:20). Such a community does not seek to be a flight from the world but a nurturing and sustaining force to transform the world. If a teacher feels alone and isolated in her Christian life, she may become discouraged and alienated from the Church. Through the community, the teacher may share in the liturgical and service dimensions of the Church. The religious community can be a source of consolation and nurturing for a religious brother or sister.

The art of teaching
The spirituality of a teacher is integral to the enterprise of teaching. A teacher's search for holiness is closely related to how he engages in teaching. Teaching is concerned with leading students to an expanding vision of the universe and through the development of skills and values which contribute to citizenship. All true education is imaginative and transcendent.

The spirituality of work is an important dimension of the art of teaching. The Greek heritage of work was that it was for the lower classes and not for the leisured classes of society. Work debased people, according to the Greeks. The Judaeo-Christian attitude to work has been ambiguous. One theme from the Bible was that it was punishment for the first sin. Another tradition is that work is an act of co-creation to continue the creativity of God in the world. Although there will be some drudgery in many work situations, the Christian teacher might work towards a position of seeing teaching as contributing to the building of a better world.

Conversion
Metanoia or conversion is a gospel imperative: 'I tell you solemnly, unless you change...' is a constant theme of Jesus. Following Jesus is being urged to turn around, to change our ways, to risk taking a step. The invitation to conversion is rather unnerving. We are safe in our securities. Most of us fear the unknown. Discipleship moves us into uncharted waters without compass or maps, only God. Frankly, we are not always sure about God. Some strange things seem to happen to followers of Jesus, or so at least, our observation tells us.

Conversion is not a one event thing, it is ongoing. Our commitment to follow the path of Jesus is a series of starts, jolts, stops and restartings. It is rarely a smooth passage. Sometimes feelings of religious joy fill our beings but most of the time it's dull plodding, holding fast to our trust in God in spite of lots of evidence to the contrary. It's little wonder that the pages of the Bible are filled with the refrain 'Don't be afraid'. Fear impedes our response to love. The epistle of John says:

> In love there can be no fear,
> but fear is driven out by perfect love (1 Jn 4:18).

Family living

Living in family is a special dimension of a teacher's spirituality. The family has been called the 'domestic Church'. Within family, the teacher is engaged in a search for intimacy and an expression of sexuality. The joys and struggles of daily living are often first experienced in family. The family provides the environment for spiritual growth and personal development. Adults and children learn the values of co-operation and hospitality. Today there are many pressures on families. Hopefully family living for a teacher will be a source of affirmation. The relational aspect of spirituality is clearly evidenced and lived in a Christian family or religious community for sisters and brothers.

Peace and justice

The history of Christian spirituality has demonstrated how readily it assumed the character of a 'flight from the world'. Monastic styles of spirituality became very individualistic in their focus. Today Christian spirituality is very concerned with a discipleship of action for justice. Johann Metz drew attention to the malaise of what he termed 'believed-in-faith', in which the rhetoric was impressive but is not translated into action. Liberation theologians, in particular, have written strongly against this 'believed-in-faith' which is rational and middle class. Such a faith was all very logical and secure but it was not founded in the life experience of struggles for freedom.

When Jesus announced the coming of the Kingdom, he demonstrated the spirit of the reign of God by his healing miracles and concern for the marginalised: 'But if it is through the finger of God that I cast out devils, then know that the Kingdom of God has overtaken you' (Lk 12:20). The finger of God pointed to the lame walking, the blind seeing, sinners being reconciled and lepers healed. The Christian way is a socially responsive Gospel. Ethical expressions are inherent in the very meaning of discipleship.

A teacher has many opportunities to promote justice. The teaching environment provides unjust situations each day. The school timetable, the home background of some children, a teacher's learning approach, a bullying parent, an excursion fee, assessment and discipline policies, may all be areas of injustice. Our own moral conversion as teachers of justice sensitises us to critique unjust situations and to act to set others free.

The prophet Micah proposes a motto for all teachers:

This is what Yahweh asks of you:
only this, to act justly,
to love tenderly,
and to walk humbly with your God (Mi 6:8).

Vision
Every teacher has a different kind of map for the spiritual life. Our personality, social environment and teaching context influence the ways we are and how we relate. Our God images have been shaped by parental and family influences. Levels of participation in the ecclesial community may vary according to past and present experiences of Church.

The vision of hope for a Christian teacher is a foundational one for spirituality. This vision includes an educational and religious dimension. It is a vision which is energised by the belief that God loves us unconditionally in Jesus. Our own personal limits and sinfulness need not crush us but can be a point of allowing us to be taken over by this forgiving love. If a teacher can let God's dream for her become more of a reality in her vocation, then the fruits of the dream are harvested in the dynamics of the teaching relationship. My plea to teachers would be:

> Hold fast to your dreams and let them grow
> Imagine the impossible with your students so
> that the possible becomes obsolete.

The vocation of the teacher is concerned with creating the image of God in our world, transforming its limits of knowledge and wisdom to serve the cause of communion in our world. Spirituality for teachers is a unifying energy which incorporates the whole of the teaching endeavour. This book is a resource for teachers to deepen the mystery of encountering God and to share this encounter through teaching. Perhaps too, this book will motivate teachers to engage in their teaching with a new enthusiasm for their magnificent vocations. Like Jesus, we teachers might be inspired to say:

> I have come to bring fire to the earth, and how I wish it were blazing already! (Lk 12:49)

Prophecy
Prophets are those who speak for God. They see more clearly and feel impelled to speak out, to denounce injustice, to challenge the status quo and explore the fallacies of our society. Prophets are discontented people. They make nuisances of themselves and are sometimes difficult to live with. They won't accept situations which are not in harmony with the ideals of the Kingdom of God. The theme of Irenaeus, 'The glory of God is the human person fully alive', is their criterion for evaluating what is happening around them.

We all possess some elements of prophecy. In a sense most teachers are 'little prophets'. At staff meetings, we may challenge existing policies on discipline or the way in which staff speak to students; we may question the cost of school excursions in economically disadvantaged environments.

We like to hold fast to bastions of security from which we won't budge. Hopefully our encounter with the God of mercy will enable us to share more fully in the prophetic mission of Christ to make our world conform more to the dream of Jesus. It is more peaceful existence not to be prophetic – people sometimes fight back with hostility and banishments. But the desire for truth and integrity flowing out of our relationship with the Lord of truth and justice will strengthen our courage. If we keep hold of the hand of Jesus in crossing the stormy seas, it's a safe passage. We begin to sink when we look down at how rough the waves are. A spirituality for Christian teachers will always contain some element of prophecy because part of a teacher's role is to lead students to enlightenment. Such a role necessitates a confrontation with oppressive situations. Prophecy leads us to new possibilities of being human.

Humour
A sense of humour is a great help in the spiritual life. Humour strips us of pretentiousness. A good laugh is a healthy remedy for our foibles and the silly things that happen. Humour puts events into perspective. It's rather humbling when we do stupid things. Humility is a recognition of our limits. Humble people enjoy a joke because they don't carry self-important illusions about themselves. The God of paradox is a God of dance and play. The Book of Proverbs expresses the God of play in these words:

> I was by his side, a master craftsman,
> delighting him day after day,
> ever at play in his presence,
> at play everywhere in the world,
> delighting to be with the sons of men (Pr 8:30-31).

Let us see the funny side of our spiritual lives. I'm sure the Lord has lots of laughs with us!

REFLECTION

1. Begin a journal for your spiritual life. Write a short reflection each week (or each day if you can) about some aspect of your spiritual journey.

2. With a friend or spiritual director evaluate your spiritual life now and the direction you seem to be taking.

3. What are you doing as a teacher to expand your Christian vision?

4. Do you belong to a Christian community? Is it a vital one? How might you gain support and affirmation from a community?

5. How is your vocation as teacher expressed in action for justice? What situations do you meet in your teaching profession which seem to be unjust? What is your response?

6. Where is the sabbath in your life?

7. What prayer practices and styles are important to you?

    How might you develop your prayer life?

8. What is the most significant image of God for you?

SCRIPTURE

Luke 6:39-45

Jesus told a parable to them, 'Can one blind man guide another? Surely both will fall into a pit? The disciple is not superior to his teacher; the fully trained disciple will always be like his teacher. Why do you observe the splinter in your brother's eye and never notice the plank in your own? How can you say to your brother, 'Brother, let me take out the splinter that is in your eye', when you cannot see the plank in your own? Hypocrite! Take the plank out of your own eye first, and then you will see clearly enough to take out the splinter that is in your brother's eye.

'There is no sound tree that produces rotten fruit, nor again a rotten tree that produces sound fruit. For every tree can be told by its own fruit: people do not pick figs from thorns, nor gather grapes from brambles. A good man draws what is good from the store of goodness in his heart; a bad man draws what is bad from the store of badness. For a man's words flow out of what fills his heart.'

Acts 4:32-35

The whole group of believers was united, heart and soul; no one claimed for his own use anything that he had, as everything they owned was held in common.

The apostles continued to testify to the resurrection of the Lord Jesus with great power, and they were all given great respect.

None of their members was ever in want, as all those who owned land or houses would sell them, and bring the money from them, to present it to the apostles; it was then distributed to any members who might be in need.

Paths and Stories

Isaiah 40:9
>Go up on a high mountain
>joyful messenger to Zion.
>Shout with a loud voice
>joyful messenger to Jerusalem.
>Shout without fear,
>say to the towns of Judah
>'there is your God'.

SAYINGS OF CONSOLATION

Yahweh, my heart has no lofty ambitions,
   my eyes do not look too high.
I am not concerned with great affairs
   or marvels beyond my scope.
Enough for me to keep my soul tranquil and quiet
   like a child in its mother's arms,
as content as a child that has been weaned (Ps 131).

A blessing on the man who puts his trust in Yahweh,
with Yahweh for his hope.
He is like a tree by the waterside
that thrusts its roots to the stream:
when the heat comes it feels no alarm,
its foliage stays green;
it has no worries in a year of drought,
and never ceases to bear fruit (Jr 17:7-8).

   Think of God's mercy, my brothers, and worship him, I beg you, in a way that is worthy of thinking beings, by offering your living bodies as a holy sacrifice, truly pleasing to God. Do not model yourselves on the behaviour of the world around you, but let your behaviour change, modelled by your new mind. This is the only way to discover the will of God and know what is good, what it is that God wants, what is the perfect thing to do (Rm 12:1-2).

BIBLIOGRAPHY

Brennan, Patrick J., *Spirituality for an Anxious Age,* 'Into your hands', The Thomas More Press, Chicago, Illinois, 1985.

Caltagirone, Carmel L., *The Catechist as Minister,* Alba House, New York, 1982.

Campbell, Alastair V., *Rediscovering Pastoral Care,* Darton, Longman & Todd, London, 1981.

de Mello, Anthony SJ, *Sadhana: A Way to God,* Gujarat Sahitya Prakash Anand, India 1978.

Doohan, Leonard, *Laity's Mission in the Local Church: Setting a New Direction,* Harper and Row, San Francisco, 1986.

Droel, William L. & Gregory, F. Augustine Pierce, *Confident and Competent: A Challenge for the Lay Church,* Ave Maria Press, Indiana, 1987.

Fallon, Michael, *Who is Jesus?* Parish Ministry Publishing 1987.

Farrell, Edward J., *Disciples and Other Strangers,* Dimension Books, New Jersey, 1974.

Farrell, Edward J., *Prayer is a Hunger,* Sheed and Ward, London, 1974.

Gallagher, Michael Paul, *Free to Believe,* Darton, Longman & Todd, London, 1987.

Garvey, John (ed.), *Modern Spirituality: An Anthology,* Darton, Longman & Todd, London, 1985.

Huelsman, Richard J., *Pray,* Paulist Press, New York, 1976.

Hughes, Gerard W., *God of Surprises,* Darton, Longman & Todd, London, 1985.

Mainosb, John, *The Present Christ,* Darton, Longman & Todd, London, 1985.

Maloney, George SJ, *Centering on the Lord Jesus,* Michael Glazier Inc., Delaware, 1983.

Nemeck, Francis Kelly OMI and Coombs, Marie Therese, Hermit, *The Spiritual Journey: Critical Thresholds and Stages of Adult Spiritual Genesis,* Michael Glazier, Delaware 1987.

Pooley, Roger & Seddon, Philip (ed.), *The Lord of the Journey,* Collins, 1986.

Sheldrake, Philip, *Images of Holiness,* Darton, Longman & Todd, London, 1987.

Van Breemen, Peter G., *Certain as the New Dawn,* Dimension Books, New Jersey, 1980.